EVERYTHING ELSE YOU ALWAYS WANTED TO KNOW ABOUT GOD

EVERYTHING

YOU ALWAYS WANTED TO KNOW ABOUT GOD

[BUT WERE AFRAID TO ASK]

ERIC METAXAS

WATERBROOK
PRESS

EVERYTHING *ELSE* YOU ALWAYS WANTED TO KNOW ABOUT GOD
(BUT WERE AFRAID TO ASK)
PUBLISHED BY WATERBROOK PRESS
12265 Oracle Boulevard, Suite 200
Colorado Springs, Colorado 80921
A division of Random House Inc.

ISBN 978-1-4000-7102-9

Library of Congress Cataloging-in-Publication Data
Metaxas, Eric.
Everything else you always wanted to know about God (but were afraid to ask) / Eric Metaxas. — 1st ed.
p. cm.
Includes bibliographical references.
ISBN 978-1-4000-7102-9
1. God (Christianity) I. Title.
BT103.M477 2007
231—dc22
2007003704

Printed in the United States of America
2007—First Edition

10 9 8 7 6 5 4 3 2 1

To everyone still childlike enough to have questions

Contents

Acknowledgments

Though it is usually difficult to understand precisely how one is influenced, it can also, in some cases, be embarrassingly easy. On the better parts of this book and its predecessor, the influence of the Reverend Tim Keller of Manhattan's Redeemer Presbyterian Church is probably so obvious to some that it hardly needs mentioning. For his unwitting participation in these pages, I am exceedingly grateful. I wish also to express my gratitude for the expert editing of Ron Lee, without whose patience, skill, and knowledge this book would not be much of a book at all. It is no small thing to see one's work influenced and improved by others, and I am grateful for that influence and improvement not just in this book but in the book to which this is a sequel.

Introduction

If you've seen a book I wrote a few years ago, *Everything You Always Wanted to Know About God (but were afraid to ask)*, you will probably see right away that this is a continuation of that earlier conversation. I suppose you could call this book a sequel or part two. If you're French, you could call it part *deux*.

But I have to say up front that the title of this book gives me hives. I don't want to start off on the wrong foot, but as the author—and, yes, I'll be your author for the rest of the book—I feel compelled to let you know that I can't possibly deliver on it. *Everything* Else *You Always Wanted to Know About God*? The title implies that every question that didn't make it into the first book will appear in this one and that after you finish this book, you'll know every single thing about God you've ever wanted to know. Something tells me that's not going to happen. Book titles can be funny that way, except as the author I'm not even snickering. If you were here, you could hear me not snickering. Or not hear me snickering. Either way.

The whole thing reminds me of when a friend told me about his grandmother's going to see the movie *Dances with Wolves.* She was hugely disappointed because in the whole picture the main character didn't dance with more than one wolf! Maybe two at the most. My friend's grandmother felt she'd been cheated—and hadn't she? She had been looking forward to the main character dancing with a whole mess of wolves! And understandably so, because the title—ahem—had raised that expectation rather explicitly. She wasn't insisting on any particular kind of dancing, but, yes, she had quite been expecting a lot of dancing with a lot of wolves, and that hadn't been the case at all. Perhaps she had pictured a big ballroom filled with wolves twirling elegantly or maybe some kind of big production number. That's what I feel you might be expecting now—and all I'm offering is the theological equivalent of a single gimpy wolf limping to a polka. You were expecting the *Ziegfeld Follies,* and all you got was the lupine version of *The Lawrence Welk Show.*

Well, there's not much I can say at this point. I'll call the printer and see if we can't fix it before too many get printed. In the meantime...*ana-one-a, ana-two-a...*

1

Who Exactly Is God?

Where God Came from; What to Call Him; How He Differs from Us (and Barry Manilow)

The world-famous New Testament scholar N. T. Wright says that when he was a young man he served as the chaplain at a university. He often encountered students who would tell him right off the bat that they didn't believe in God, hoping to be rid of him for the next four years. But Wright wouldn't let them off the hook so easily. "Which God don't you believe in?" he would ask. This usually took them by surprise and got them to think for a minute. Most of them then described the God they didn't believe in. Almost always this non-God was something of a dyspeptic, white-bearded curmudgeon who sat on a cloud and hurled thunderbolts at anyone who seemed to be having fun. Wright would listen to their description and then respond that he didn't believe in that God either. A conversation often ensued in which the idea of who God really is—and who God isn't—was more deeply explored.[1]

Q: Before I ask you who God is, could I ask you another question first?

A: Of course! You can ask anything you want, remember? That's the whole point of the book!

Q: Okay. Where did God come from?

A: Um, actually, I meant to say you can ask any question *except that one.*

Q: Why? If we assume God exists, it shouldn't be hard to explain where he came from.

A: Well, no one knows for sure, but we're looking into it. Okay?

Q: Already with the joking?

A: What if I told you we suspect he came from Canada?

Q: Can you be serious?

A: Sorry. But this is one of those frustrating questions that elude an easy answer. Even to *try* answering it, I have to get into some heavy concepts. I just feel it's a little early in the book to get so heavy.

Q: If it gets too heavy, I can always skip ahead to the next section, can't I?

A: I suppose so.

Q: Well?

A: Okay, here goes. The first thing we have to understand when we ask a question like where did God come from is that God exists outside of time and space.[2] In fact, in case you hadn't heard, he created time and space.

Q: Yes, I'd heard that.

A: And of course we exist *inside* time and space. So if God is outside time and space, and we are inside them, then trying to figure out where God came from gets pretty complicated. It's certainly more complicated than trying to figure out where, say, Barry Manilow was born.

Q: Then I'll assume Barry Manilow is not God?

A: Not that Barry Manilow is not an amazing performer! But, no, he's not God. And so when we're talking about God and where he came from, we can't just say Canada or Paramus. It's not that simple. However, there is one thing we *can* say, and that is that God always existed. He existed before time existed and before the universe existed. He had to, since he's the one who created time and space. He's eternal, and he exists in eternity, which is a completely different dimension, if not several other dimensions.

Q: Okay, so what kind of a world was it before time and space existed?

A: I'm not sure there was a world. But whatever it was like, we know there were no watches.

Q: Because there was no time.

A: Bingo. And no closets, because there was no space. Ha. But beyond that, we're kind of stumped. On this question, we face almost exactly the same difficulty that scientists face in trying to understand what existed before the so-called Big Bang, which is when they say time and space began.

Q: And who or what do they say was behind the Big Bang?

A: They can be very touchy on that subject. Let's just say it happened, okay?

Q: But what were you saying about scientists being stumped by what happened before time and space existed?

A: I was saying that scientists can theoretically look back to the very first fraction of a fraction of a second when the Big Bang happened—and can describe what the universe was like in its first few moments. But they can't go back *before* then. They hit a wall, so to speak. It's what scientists call a "singularity," a point beyond which it's impossible to go. And to get back to your question about where God came from, when we look for an answer to that question, we hit a similar wall.

Q: So we're stuck.

A: Yes. You and I can't see before the beginning of time and space any more than a scientist can. But we can know that, according to the Bible, God existed before then because he exists outside time and space.

Q: You were right. This is kind of heavy for the beginning of the book.

A: Well, you could have skipped ahead.

Q: Okay, now that we got that out of the way, who exactly is God?

A: In one sense, this is an odd question. God is God. But so many people mean different things when they say "God" that it's important to clarify his identity if we can.

Q: Right. So who is he?

A: Well, I assume we're talking about the God of the Bible, and the God of the Bible actually has many names. Usually he's called Jehovah, which is just another way of saying Yahweh.

Q: But can't I use whatever name I like? And why do I even have to use the word God? What about Energy or The Force or something like that?

A: First of all, if we're talking about the God of the Bible, we're talking about a God for whom names are extremely important. In fact, in a few places in the Bible, when something significant happens to a person, God gives that person a new name. In the book of Genesis, after God reveals himself to Abram, he changes Abram's name to Abraham. And in the New Testament, Jesus tells Simon that his new name will be Peter, which means "rock."[3] Those are just two examples. Names have a lot of meaning in the Bible, so we'd have to assume that God wants us to take his name seriously too.

Q: If you say so.

A: In fact, many Jewish people take God's name so seriously that they won't even write or say the word *Yahweh,* because for them the name of God is holy. They can write it without the vowels, using just the four consonants, but they will never write out the whole word.

Q: But Christians are free to say it and write it?

A: Yes, but for Christians too, God's name is holy. In the Lord's Prayer, when Jesus prays to God the Father, he says, "Hallowed be thy name."[4] *Hallowed* is another word for "holy," so Jesus himself is pointing out that God's name is holy and that we should acknowledge that when we pray. We'll come back to what holiness means later, but the point is that we are supposed to take God's name very seriously. There is power in every name, and especially in God's name. In the Old Testament, it was said that the one who comes "in the name of the LORD" is blessed,[5] and when Jesus entered Jerusalem before he was crucified, the people lining the streets identified him as "he who comes in the name of the Lord!"[6] If you're around Christians, you will often hear them pray "in Jesus' name." The name itself has power and authority.

If you were in a country that had a monarchy and someone said, "I come in the name of the king!" his words would have the same effect as if the king himself were standing there. His authority would be present in an emissary who comes in the king's name. It's just like that when we use the name of God. God's authority is somehow present in his name, which is another reason the Ten Commandments forbid taking God's name in vain.[7] God's name is too holy and too important to throw around lightly.

Q: While we're on the subject, what exactly does it mean to "take God's name in vain"?

A: Most folks think it means swearing, but taking God's name in vain means using God's name lightly—whether you say "Jesus!" when you slam your finger in a car door or whether you simply say "God!" when you are horrified at something. If we really understood how holy and powerful God's name is, we would never use it lightly, or "take his name in vain," to use the old-fashioned term.

As I said, this goes far beyond swearing. We are supposed to revere God's name, but most people in our culture have completely lost sight of what that means. The Bible makes it very clear that there is power in God's name. Demons tremble and cower at God's name.[8] You have to wonder what they know that we don't.

Q: I understand the idea that God's name is important. But I'm still not sure why he can't be called whatever we want to call him.

A: One reason is that God can't be whoever we want him to be. We have to know who we're talking about when we're talking about God. He can't be some entity that we've made up, a God created in our own image, so to speak. He's real; he's not just an idea. But let's try something. Tell me who you have in mind when you're talking about God, and maybe we can figure out who you mean.

Q: Well, I know that if he's God, he has to be good. And loving. And he has to be fair.

A: That rules out calling him Satan, right? Or Lucifer or Mephistopheles or Beelzebub. Just in case you wondered if any of those names might qualify. You see how names are important?

Okay, what else would you say to describe God?

Q: He's kind, and he cares deeply about the poor and the suffering.

A: Okay, that rules out most Hindu gods.

Q: Really?

A: Yes, absolutely. It also rules out the ancient Greek and Roman gods and the Egyptian gods. In fact, it rules out all the pagan gods. Zeus and Thoth and Ra and Neptune and Mars and Venus and that whole gang are not on any level interested in the poor and the suffering. What else?

Q: When I say "God," I'm thinking about someone who cares about me—and keeps his eye on me.

A: Well, that definitely rules out The Force or any impersonal deities along those lines, which are closer to a kind of Eastern or New Age version of God. Eastern religions and New Age religions don't have in mind a God who is a person and who created us in his image. Their idea of God isn't a deity who knows you and knows what you're going through and cares about your difficulties. So far the God you're describing is definitely the God of the Bible. No other God meets your description. And as I said earlier, his name is Jehovah and Yahweh. He has a lot of other names, but the bottom line is that now we know who we are talking about and who we're not talking about.

Q: What does Jehovah mean? Or Yahweh?

A: In the book of Exodus when Moses encounters the burning bush and talks to God, Moses asks God who he is. In giving his name, God speaks the Hebrew word *Yahweh*—what we sometimes call *Jehovah*. It is best translated as "I AM" or "I AM WHO I AM."[9]

Q: That's not much of a translation. In fact it sounds more like a riddle than a name.

A: It really is hard to translate, but *Yahweh* means something like "I am who I am" or "he who will always be."

Q: That doesn't do much to clear this up.

A: Well, all these phrases carry the superimportant idea that God is self-existent and eternal, which takes us back to where we started. He's the God who is outside time and space and who has always existed. But he communicates with us, who are inside time and space. That right there is really at the core of who God is. He's the God who leaves eternity and enters time because he wants to connect with us—whom he loves. It's all through the Bible. We see it happening when he tells Abram to leave his home and set out on a journey to who knows where. And we see it when Moses encounters God at the burning bush.[10] Of course, we see it most obviously and most dramatically when Jesus came into the world. When Jesus entered time and space, he changed human history forever. It's all pretty heavy, the more you think about it.

Q: Heavier than I thought, that's for sure.

A: It's crucial to know that God is real and that he can't and won't be just whoever we want him to be. It's up to each of us to find out who he is and what he's like. The idea is that we are supposed to get to know him and become more and more like him. But instead of doing that, we sometimes try to make God more like us. That's backward. He is who he is, and what we want him to be or not be isn't going to change him. Unlike, say, Mr. Potato Head.

Q: Okay, how exactly is God not like Mr. Potato Head?

A: With Mr. Potato Head, we accept the basic shape, but the rest is up to us. And of course we make him look the way we want by putting on whichever hat and glasses and eyebrows we like best.

Q: I always use the little pipe.

A: Whatever. The point is that we're supposed to do that with Mr. Potato Head, but if we try it with God, it won't work. We can't say, "I like the part about his being good and just and loving, so I'll start there. But I'll change the part about his telling me what to do with my body or telling me that all religions aren't equal." With God, we have to take the whole package. If he truly is God, and if he loves us and knows us, then we can trust him with the things that might puzzle us or rub us the wrong way. If he's God, we have to deal with him as he is, not as we want him to be.

Q: But just handing over control to a God you can't even see can be a bit frightening.

A: Right, but if we don't, we are effectively saying that we're in control, which is like putting ourselves in God's place. If we want to know who God is, we have to understand that we're not him. We answer to God, not vice versa. But the good news is that he really is God. So we can relax and trust him. He is the source of all beauty and joy and goodness and truth and justice. So even if there is something about the God of the Bible that makes us uncomfortable, we can still trust him with the things we're not sure about.

If he's really God, we can let him challenge us and change us, and we can know that we'll be moving in the right direction, toward being more like God, becoming more full of love and truth and justice.

Q: So we've determined that I'm not God.

A: Yes. And of course we've also determined that Barry Manilow—great as he is—is not God.

Knowing who God is *not* can be the most important step toward understanding who God really is. Many of us spend years feeling resentful or indifferent toward a God who, in the end, never existed at all. If not for the joy of eventually discovering who God really is, it could all be very embarrassing.

2

Does God Still Throw Thunderbolts?

God's Wrath; Fearing God; God's Love for Us

Theologian John Rankin often gets audience members' attention by claiming that the Bible says God has a long nose. And he's not kidding. The Bible does say just that, in the original Hebrew of the Old Testament. It's one of those places where a phrase is not meant literally but rather as a figure of speech. And it's not referring to God's facial features but rather to a subject familiar to anyone who's read the Old Testament: God's wrath.

In order to understand how the phrase "God has a long nose" relates to God's wrath, we first have to know that in ancient Israel all men wore beards—and tended to have more than a little facial hair in general. In English if we say someone got "red in the face," we mean the person was angry. But in the ancient Hebrew culture, you couldn't say that. Men's faces were so covered with facial hair that you wouldn't notice their cheeks turning red. The only part of their face that you could see turn red would be their nose. So "having a long nose" became a euphemism for someone who took a long time to get angry. Of course, many English translations of the Bible say God is "slow to anger," but the original Hebrew text simply says God "has a long nose."[1] This doesn't mean God never gets angry, but it does mean that, like the most loving father we can imagine, he has a lot of grace toward us. To use another euphemism, we might say God is not a hot-head. I don't know which euphemism you prefer, but in either case, it's good news.

Q: Okay, I know God isn't some cranky old guy on a cloud throwing thunderbolts. But are you sure he doesn't use natural disasters to punish us? Because I keep hearing that he does.

A: Can you be more specific?

Q: I've heard religious leaders say that God used a hurricane or a tsunami or some other disaster to punish people for their particular sins. Is that true?

A: In a word: no. In three words: no, no, no, no!

Q: That was four words.

A: I know. I got carried away.

Q: Okay, but if God doesn't do that, then why do people keep saying that he does? Some people say God is wonderful and loves us, and others say he's vengeful and will punish his enemies whenever they step out of line.

A: Of course there is truth to the idea that there is justice in the world, so those who turn away from God turn away from his love and grace—and will reap the negative consequences of that. But when we claim to know the details of how that all works and start announcing that a particular disaster was God's response to a specified sin, we are skating on very thin ice. In fact, when we link those sorts of things, we are directly contradicting what Jesus himself said on the subject.

Q: Jesus said we shouldn't blame disasters on the sins of certain people?

A: Absolutely. It's in the gospel of Luke, chapter 13. And if someone is teaching the opposite of what Jesus says on the subject, maybe that person should worry about his own sins instead of the sins of other people.

Q: Okay, what does Jesus say on the subject, and why are these religious leaders—who claim to know the Bible and to follow Jesus—saying what they're saying?

A: Let's take one question at a time. First of all, yes, Jesus says it's flat-out wrong for us to conclude that those who are killed in a tragedy are being punished for their guilt. In the gospel of Luke, some people ask Jesus whether God punishes sinners directly, with dramatic acts of retribution. And Jesus references something that must have happened not long before in a neighboring town. A tower had collapsed, and eighteen people were killed. Jesus says, "Those eighteen who died when the tower in Siloam fell on them—do you think they were more guilty than all the others living in Jerusalem?"[2]

Q: And?

A: And then he promptly answers his own question. "I tell you, no!" he says. And then, to drive his point home, he adds, "But unless you repent, you too will all perish."[3]

Q: So what's the point?

A: The point is that pointing our finger at others and blaming them that way is wrong. Because it misses the most important point of all, which is that we are *all* guilty. Jesus says we must first be aware of our own guilt before we have any business thinking about someone else's guilt. There's another famous passage where Jesus says that before we worry about the speck of sawdust in someone else's eye, we should worry about the plank of lumber in our own eye![4]

The point is that you and I and everyone else are terribly guilty by God's standards, and we all should look at our own guilt first. If we are thoroughly aware of how guilty we are, we will have much more grace and love and understanding for others and for their sins. That's exactly how God wants it. It's not that we shouldn't worry about sins in general, but we should start by being concerned about our own. That's at the core of the Christian faith.

So to get back to your question, Jesus makes it very clear that those who suffer, who are hurt or killed in any type of tragedy or disaster, are not necessarily more guilty than anyone else.

Q: But how can so many high-profile religious leaders miss something that Jesus himself talks about?

A: First of all, it's a problem of human nature. All of us have a tendency to point out the faults of others before we point out our own. For example, right this minute most of us love the idea of demonizing the religious folks who get on television and make these statements. Am I right? Be honest!

Q: Now that you mention it, yes. I admit it. I do enjoy pointing out that they are hypocrites.

A: And isn't that a little hypocritical? But Jesus' main point is that we are *all* hypocrites. We need to look at our own faults first. We all have a desire to feel superior to others, and that's at the heart of what sin is all about. It's moral pride, in the negative sense of the word.

Q: I hadn't thought of that.

A: Don't feel bad. Obviously the religious leaders who claim to know that God used a hurricane to punish certain sinners haven't either. But we all get this wrong. We all want to feel morally superior. We point the finger at someone else, as if that gets us off the hook. But pointing out the sins of others doesn't get anyone off the hook about their own sins. And pointing out the hypocrisy in religious leaders doesn't help either. God just looks at us and says, "Yes, you're right. Those others are sinful and hypocritical. Now what about *your* sins and hypocrisy?"

Q: Okay, I see your point. But I'm still curious about where religious leaders who teach the Bible would get that idea if Jesus spoke out against it.

A: They get it from a few places. Probably the main place is the Old Testament and the many stories of how God dealt with ancient Israel. But that was a completely different situation.

Q: How was it different?

A: God had a unique relationship with ancient Israel, so his dealings with the Israelites can't be considered normative for all people and all times. Whenever the people of Israel turned their backs on God, they were visited with repercussions. But God warned them beforehand. They knew in advance that if they rebelled against God, they were opening themselves up to all manner of tragic circumstances, which included being sold into slavery for four hundred years, being attacked by enemies, losing military battles, and wandering in the desert for forty years. But this cause-and-effect relationship was not something that someone discovered afterward. God had made it explicit that this was how he would deal with his people.

Q: But that type of divine punishment applied only to ancient Israel?

A: Right. When we are talking about the world in general, that model cannot hold. The rest of the world isn't in a relationship with God in the way that ancient Israel was. To casually point to natural disasters as evidence of God's punishing people is just one step away from saying to someone who has stubbed a toe, "Ha! God got you!" It's childish and simplistic—and theologically just plain wrong. But the worst thing about that kind of thinking is that it paints God as some kind of neighborhood bully dispensing vigilante justice. God isn't like that. He is our perfect, loving Father, and to characterize him as anything else is a terrible mistake.

Q: So when Jesus commented on the disaster of the falling tower, he was trying to get people to stop blaming natural disasters on particular sinners?

A: It's pretty amazing, isn't it? The idea that the Bible gives us Jesus' own words on the subject. It reminds me of that scene in *Annie Hall* where Woody Allen is waiting in line at a movie theater. The character he is playing, Alvy Singer, is having an argument with someone about the writings of Marshall McLuhan. Finally Alvy has had enough. He says that he's going to prove he's right and says that Marshall McLuhan himself will settle it once and for all. Sure enough, Alvy grabs Marshall McLuhan, who is also waiting in the line, and McLuhan agrees that Alvy is right and says the person he's arguing with has no idea what he's talking about. It's a beautiful moment.[5]

Q: So God is concerned about our sin and hypocrisy, but he doesn't send hurricanes or other disasters to punish people who are especially wicked. But if God is all love and hugs, then why do we hear so much about how we are supposed to fear him?

A: Good question! But who said God is all love and hugs? It's true that God is all-loving, but even the most loving parent dispenses justice to kids who step out of line. We have to remember that God is slow to anger, but he's full of justice too. He's the ultimate Judge of the universe. That's a far cry from being some sort of cosmic teddy bear.

Q: Still, the idea of fearing God sounds so negative. Why would I want anything to do with a God who says I have to fear him? It makes him sound like he has a huge ego.

A: I can see why you'd think that, but actually the opposite is true. God is all love, which is the *opposite* of ego. The idea of a God who wants us to fear him might sound like a God who is self-centered, but it's not. God is fundamentally and radically *other*-centered. That's what love is about. But this is a bit beside the point.

Q: What <u>is</u> the point?

A: The point is that the idea of fearing God isn't a negative thing at all. We have the wrong idea about what that phrase means. When the Bible talks about fearing God, it's a very different meaning of the word *fear.* God doesn't want us to cringe in fear of him, which would imply that he means us harm and that we fundamentally dislike him. The idea of fearing God has gotten distorted over time, as many ideas about God have.

Q: How so?

A: Just think of the phrase "God-fearing folk." It brings to mind grim, prune-faced characters who glower at others and wear dark, old-fashioned clothing and think that smiling or dancing is on par with witchcraft and conjuring—people who think playing gin rummy or even crazy eights is on par with voodoo and hoodoo…

Q: And?

A: And the idea of fearing God has nothing whatsoever to do with that sort of thing. Fearing God has much more to do with the idea of awe than with fear.

Q: Awe?

A: Yes, the concept of fearing God is much closer to meaning "being in awe of" or "standing in awe of." But there can be a kind of terror and fear to awe too. It's the idea of being in the presence of something so huge or so overwhelming and powerful that you take it very seriously. Imagine being in a rowboat far out from shore and a blue whale surfaces near you. You don't just shrug. You stare at it in awe. You sit up and take notice. You respect the size and majesty and power of what you are looking at. Fearing God is something like that, except much more so, because God created whales. And the vast oceans they swim in. And the planet to whose surface the oceans cling. And all the planets and all the stars in our galaxy. And in all the other hundred billion galaxies that we know of.

Q: Got it.

A: The idea of fearing God also has something to do with respecting him, which in part has to do with respecting what he tells us and therefore doing what he tells us to do. He doesn't want us to listen to him because he needs his ego stroked but because he loves us and wants the best for us. He wants us to thrive and to avoid calamity. So he tells us what behavior will bless us and what behavior will harm us. But he can't force us to listen to him. It's up to us to regard God with enough awe that we pay attention to what he says. If we know how infinitely wise and loving he is, we won't take lightly what he says. We couldn't possibly.

God isn't trying to prevent anyone from having a good time; he's trying to prevent us from having a bad time. But even this makes it sound like fearing God or obeying him is all about avoiding trouble. It's about *much more* than that. There is a hugely positive side to it too. And that is the real point of it all.

Q: So what's the positive side?

A: It gets back to what we touched on a moment ago. God is so big and unfathomable that to really see him as he is—in all his majesty and universe-creating power and mystery—is far beyond us. Just to get the smallest glimpse of him as he really is would be too much for us to bear.

Q: And this is positive?

A: Hang on. I'm not done. I mentioned seeing a huge whale up close when you're on the ocean in a rowboat. Can you think of anything that ever stopped you in your tracks, something that took your breath away?

Q: I once saw a '63 Vette in mint condition. Original paint job and—wait for it—original interior.

A: I was hoping you might come up with something even more amazing than that, maybe something that wasn't manufactured at a Chevy plant.

Q: Okay. I'm thinking.

A: While you're thinking, the best example I can think of is the Grand Canyon. Many people say that seeing the Grand Canyon is a powerfully awesome experience, but it's hard to know why. It certainly has something to do with its extreme size, coupled with its overwhelming beauty. Many people say they want to cry, and many people do cry. But we have to wonder what it is about the Grand Canyon that has that effect on people.

Q: What do you think it is?

A: I think there's something inside us that knows God is real. And somehow we know that he's so huge we can't imagine him or fully take him in and that he's so beautiful it would make us cry to see him up close. And when we see something like the Grand Canyon, we get a glimpse of that. Even when we don't know what it is we're feeling, we know that our hearts leap.

And it's not just the size and the beauty; it has something to do with the fact that we are so small in comparison. Suddenly we are in the presence of something so big and so beautiful that we forget about ourselves. It's as if we are taken out of ourselves and are drawn into the vastness and the beauty of the thing we are looking at, and we don't know why, but it breaks our heart. We know, somehow, that we are glimpsing God.

Q: But it's not God. It's a huge hole in the ground.

A: Of course it's not God. But through it we are catching a glimpse of God's majesty. Even if we aren't consciously aware of it, we stand in awe of what we see because a part of us, the part that knows that God is real but that almost dares not think about it, responds. It's like a person who hasn't been touched by another human being in a long, long time. If that person is suddenly hugged by another human, he very likely will start crying.

The part of us that knows God exists is longing to feel his touch. Then something happens, like seeing the vastness and beauty of the Grand Canyon, and we feel God's fingers brushing against us. When we see anything beautiful, and especially when we see something as overwhelming and awesome as the Grand Canyon, the part of us that has almost lost all hope is reminded that God really exists, that it's true. And we cry.

Q: So God isn't all love and hugs, as you say, but he is all-loving. That makes me wonder: if God loves everybody in the world, then what's the big deal about it?

A: What?

Q: If God loves <u>everybody</u>, then why is it such a big deal that he loves me? Loving people is just what he does, right? He's indiscriminate about it, and he loves billions of people, so forgive me if I don't feel as though I should be bowled over by it.

A: Oh, I think I see what you mean. But the problem is that you are forgetting that God is God.

Q: How does that change anything?

A: You're characterizing him as if he were a human, with our human tendencies and limitations. You're saying he can only love the way you or I love.

Q: And?

A: And that's not true. God can love six billion people as intensely as you or I could love just one person. Actually, much more than we could love only one person. He has so much love that it doesn't get diluted over six billion people or six quadrillion or whatever number you want to throw at him. He's infinite—which, in case you didn't know, is very, very, very big. And his love is infinite. Hard to imagine, I know.

Q: It is.

A: So when God says he loves everyone, it's not mushy and meaningless, as when some celebrity says it about his or her fans in an issue of *People*. With God it's real. And to prove it, he backs it up. If you were a fan of some celebrity who'd claimed to love all his or her fans, and you were to approach that celebrity, they wouldn't know who you were, much less actually care about you. You're just one of a million nameless fans. When humans say things like "I love you all so much!" they're just mouthing platitudes; there is nothing real behind it.

Q: You're saying that God is different—he really does love all his fans?

A: God doesn't have fans. God created us, which means we're much more than just fans; we are his beloved children. So even if someone doesn't know who God is, or even if a person hates God, God still loves that person with a love we can't imagine. He knows each of us and loves us intimately and with such intensity we couldn't bear to know it in its full magnitude. We couldn't handle it; that's how powerful his love is.

Q: But it's still hard to understand how he could love every person on the planet individually.

A: From our human perspective it's very hard to grasp, because humans can't love like that. But God is God. The fact that he loves so many people doesn't diminish the intensity of his love at all. Remember that God is outside of time and space. If he can see the whole universe at once, and can see the past, present, and future all at once, he can probably love each one of us individually without too much stress.

Q: I think I'm getting it...

A: One more thing: when we talk about God's love, we are talking about the love by which we define all other love. God's love is everything you could ever hope or dream love to be—and infinitely more. And that means that if God says he loves you, he loves *you* and not just the people standing in the general direction of you. He means you specifically. And to paraphrase that famous line from Dante's *The Divine Comedy*, it's the love that moves the sun and moon and stars.

Q: It's unfathomable, but it's also personal?

A: Yes, that's part of what's so amazing about it. God's love is so vast it created the universe, but it's also intensely personal. Of course, all real love is personal. God desperately wants each of us to know how much he loves us so we will accept his love. He wants nothing more than for all people to live their lives in the knowledge of his intense love. He knows that if we know his love, it will change our attitude toward ourselves and everyone else, and it will make it possible for us to live the life he created us to live.

Q: So if we don't accept God's love for us, we can't live the life we are supposed to be living?

A: Correct. When people know they are passionately loved by the God who made the universe, they will behave very differently than if they didn't know it. That's one way you can tell if someone really knows God—it changes their behavior, often rather dramatically. It's much harder to be self-centered and self-important and insecure when you really understand that God loves you.

We know that God doesn't literally have a long nose, but the idea that the awesome Creator of the universe is willing to let us think of him that way is deeply touching. The God of the Bible will go to the greatest lengths to communicate his love to us and to win our hearts. But sometimes he doesn't have to go very far at all, and in this case you might say that he wins us by a nose.

3

Why Shouldn't People Blame God for Tsunamis?

Where Evil Came from; God's Holiness; Who to Blame for Suffering

Most of us know there's something wrong with the world, something that's not easily fixed. When a group of young men flew jets carrying innocent passengers into the World Trade Center towers in lower Manhattan, our worst fears about the existence of actual evil seemed confirmed. The image of those charred, smoking stumps filled with doomed mothers and fathers is not easily erased.

The Reverend B. J. Weber has given most of his life to New York City, ministering to prostitutes and addicts in Times Square as well as to their more polished counterparts on Wall Street. When 9/11 hit, Weber found himself in an armory on lower Lexington Avenue ministering to those who were searching for loved ones. Armed with nothing more than the love of Christ and a list of the confirmed dead, Weber found himself talking with a distraught Hispanic woman whose husband's name was on the list. How can one comfort such a victim of evil? Weber hugged the woman and prayed with her. As this new widow was weeping, a well-meaning social worker stepped in, putting a pill between the woman's lips. It was an antianxiety drug. Surprised at the intrusion, the grieving woman took the pill out of her mouth. "I don't want drugs," she said. "I want to pray."[1]

Q: Okay, let's cut to the chase. Every time something good happens, you hear people thanking God for it. But when bad things happen, it's rare to hear people openly blaming him. For example, professional athletes often thank God for their victories, but they never blame him when they lose. Please explain.

A: The short answer is that God is the author of all that is good in the universe, but he's not the author of anything bad or evil.

Q: I'm afraid that's not going to cut it. Can you elaborate? If God is all-powerful and also good, how do you explain evil? I'm not trying to be blasphemous here, but how is God not responsible? If he doesn't make earthquakes and tsunamis happen, who does?

A: Well, there's a simple answer to that question, but I'm not sure you'll like it.

Q: Try me.

A: We do.

Q: Pardon me?

A: We do. You and I.

Q: We're the ones responsible for tornadoes and floods and landslides?

A: That's about the situation, I'm afraid. At least that's the short version.

Q: Just to clarify: Do you cause the tornadoes and I cause the floods, or vice versa? And who causes avalanches? Is that one of us too, or is there a third troublemaker in all this mayhem?

A: Very funny. I didn't mean you and me *literally.* I meant you and me and everyone who has ever lived. I meant you and me as in "the whole human race."

Q: I still don't see how humans are responsible for destructive forces of nature and all the other terrible things in the world.

A: We're the ones who invited evil into the world. God created a world without sin in it. It was all good. It was paradise. But we opened the door and let the bad stuff come in.

Q: Okay, I see where you're headed. You're going to talk about the apple and the serpent and the moral weakness of Adam and Eve, aren't you?

A: How did you guess?

Q: Then I've got you cornered. Because if evil was right there in the Garden of Eden so that all Adam and Eve had to do was open the door and let it in, didn't God create it in the first place? If it was

about to be unleashed, it already had to be lurking around, just waiting for Eve to take a bite out of that apple. So evil already had to exist. Am I wrong?

A: If it actually happened that way, you'd be absolutely right. But I see now that I added to your confusion by using a misleading metaphor. I shouldn't have said that we opened the door and let the bad stuff come in—by which, of course, I meant sin and death. Can I try a more accurate metaphor?

Q: I certainly wouldn't stop you.

A: Okay, let me put it this way. Adam and Eve had free will, meaning that their obedience to God was a choice. To obey God is to love him, and love by definition is something we do freely or not at all. We can't love just because we were programmed to love or because we were forced into it. Then it wouldn't be love. So when God gave Adam and Eve free will—which gave them the freedom to love him—he also gave them the ability to *not* love him, along with the ability to disobey him. That's the way love and free will work.

When Adam and Eve chose to turn away from God, evil came into the picture, and sin entered the world. But God didn't create evil; he created love. And somehow love, because of its voluntary nature, contains the possibility of evil but not evil itself. The *possibility* of evil existed in the Garden of Eden, and when Adam and Eve chose disobedience, evil was conceived. I know this is philosophical, but it's extremely important!

Q: So by turning away from God, mankind lit the fuse on evil and wrecked the universe. Is that about it?

A: Exactly.

Q: I don't see how something can contain the possibility of evil but not evil itself.

A: That's the tough part. The explanation starts with the concept that Adam and Eve disobeyed God and suddenly—whoops—they'd created a problem that was way beyond their ability to contain or remedy. It was as though they had unleashed a deadly virus, and it spread and spread and is still spreading. But let's see if another metaphor can make this at least a little bit clearer.

Q: I'm listening.

A: Imagine a harmless chemical contained in a test tube in a certain city. In a different test tube in another part of the city is another chemical, also harmless. Each of the chemicals can be used to produce tremendous good—to cure diseases, for example. That's why they were created. The good they can do is amazing. But there's one catch. If somehow the two are combined, havoc will be unleashed. The person who created the two beneficial chemicals would never ever put them together, knowing the monstrous harm that would be done. But if someone else combined them, the horror would be unleashed, and that person would be the one to blame. *Especially* if that person had been clearly told *not* to combine them.

Q: I see what you're saying, but why wouldn't stronger safeguards have been put in place to prevent combining the chemicals?

A: Yes, that's the question exactly. And we can only guess at the answers, which is definitely unsatisfying. But maybe the metaphor of human life is even more helpful in explaining it.

Q: I'm still listening.

A: Imagine one sperm and one egg. These are just two cells. There are zillions of them in existence, and none of them by itself constitutes human life, right?

Q: Right.

A: But if you put them together—*shazam!*—suddenly the two nonhuman entities can combine to become a human being. Under the right circumstances and with just the right conditions, they could become a human. The possibility is there.

Q: Absolutely.

A: Suddenly two things that are *not* human combine to produce a human. A whole new creature with a certain hair color and a certain smile and a certain way of looking to the left when thinking about a difficult problem comes into being. You can quibble about the details, but you get the idea.

Q: Sure...

A: So I could say, "Here is a vial containing a sperm, and there is a vial containing an ovum. Do not, under any circumstances, let them get together, because if you do, they will spawn something completely new and unknown—and the whole universe will be changed forever." You'd realize that you had been given an incredible responsibility.

Q: I'd certainly say so.

A: The person who gave you the two vials did not give you new human life, but only the *potential* to create human life. You're not holding a new human being; you're just holding two cells contained in separate vials. And it's exactly the same with Adam and Eve eating the apple. God put two people in a world where there was no evil. But because they were free to exercise their will and to disobey God's will, they had the potential to produce evil. It really is a frightening thought when you think about it.

Q: I'll say. So when you said earlier that you and I are responsible for earthquakes and tsunamis, you really meant to blame Adam and Eve.

A: Well, yes, they started it. But somehow we all share in their guilt. There's an old saying: "In Adam's fall, we sinned all." That about says it. We inherited a basic predisposition to disobey God. But there's one further and exceedingly important result of the Fall. You see, all of creation fell too. Not just human beings, but the *entire universe.* So the violence of nature, from weather to earthquakes to animals that eat us, is all a part of the Fall that we caused. It's pretty amazing that God gave mere humans the ability to wreck the universe. It's a bit freaky when I say it that way, but it's true. He created us and gave us an ability that he has not given to anything else, an ability to do something that affects everything else in the entire universe. Like it or not, we are that important.

Q: And because we're so important the universe has been somehow wrecked?

A: Essentially. The entire universe was somehow changed—and not for the better—as a result of that first sin. It's as if humanity took the stage at the start of a beautiful, perfect play. And instead of following God's script, we kicked down the scenery and poured water on the head of the orchestra conductor, and everyone ran screaming from the theater. And now here we are, in an empty, wrecked theater.

Q: You make it sound pretty bleak.

A: Well, yes. The Fall is bleakness itself! Which is why God's decision to redeem us from our fallen state is unfathomably beautiful. The idea that he wanted to save us from ourselves, from what we've done, is just overwhelming. It's tough to take in, because we know we don't deserve it, but he loves us that much.

Q: With you and me and Adam and Eve and everybody else responsible for wrecking the universe, doesn't it follow that maybe God isn't all that excited about letting us into heaven?

A: On the contrary, he desperately *wants* us to get into heaven. He wants to bring us there, if we'll let him. Because after the Fall, we certainly can't get there on our own. But there is no hope of that happening based on how wonderful we are. We certainly can't get there on our own merits.

Q: You're saying there's no hope, and that God's excited. You've lost me.

A: There is no hope that we can make it on our own merits. But that doesn't mean there is no hope whatsoever. In this case, God has come to our aid. He can't allow us to come into his presence as we are. Because of the Fall, we've been tainted by what's usually called "original sin"—and God is holy. So God has to somehow make it all possible.

Q: This is starting to bring back stories from Sunday school, where God's holiness was closely linked to his wrath. As I remember the story, God can't tolerate anything that isn't holy—like you and me.

A: Bingo. But saying it like that makes God sound intolerant. The fact is that we are the ones who blew it. Let's look at it this way. Yes, God is holy. And because we aren't, because we've been tainted by the Fall, we would be destroyed if we got near his holiness. It would be like landing a plane on the sun.

Q: Ouch.

A: So God has to somehow shield us from himself. He has to protect us from being fried, so to speak.

Q: Pardon?

A: The Bible says God's holiness is a consuming fire.[2] So God has to shield us from himself, from his own holiness. And that's exactly what Jesus did. He "took the heat" for us, to continue the metaphor. Jesus came to earth and stepped between us and God. And as long as we accept his "taking the heat" for our sins, we can enter God's presence, meaning we can go to heaven.

Q: I've never heard it put that way before.

A: There's a lot more to it. The Bible says that Jesus, who was sinless, became sin.[3] It's a mind-boggling concept. Jesus, who is God, left heaven and became a human being. Then, when he was hanging on the cross, he became the embodiment of all that is unholy. Very hard to fathom, but that's what the Bible says. At that point he was completely separated from God the Father. It's heartbreaking, but the truth is that he was destroyed by God's holiness so that we wouldn't be. That's God's way of letting us into heaven, even with all our failings. You've heard the statement that Jesus paid the price for our sins, and that's exactly what happened.

Q: Isn't this idea only found in the New Testament?

A: Not at all. The concept is definitely found in the Old Testament. Have you heard of the ark of the covenant?

Q: Refresh my memory.

A: If you saw *Raiders of the Lost Ark,* you'll remember it. It was the fancy wooden box that carried the two tablets on which the Ten Commandments were inscribed. Because of what it contained, the ark of the covenant was itself so holy that no one was allowed to touch it. If you touched it, you would die. That's why the Israelites carried it using two long poles, but at one point someone slipped up and touched the ark—and died instantly.[4]

Q: You're not making this up, are you?

A: Absolutely not. Anyway, the two tablets inside the ark, the ones on which the Ten Commandments were written, represented "the Law," meaning God's Law. It's the moral yardstick by which God measures us. You're with me so far?

Q: I think so.

A: Okay, in the Old Testament we read about a very important ritual in which the high priest would put sacrificial blood on the top of the ark, which was called the mercy seat. The sacrificial blood came from an innocent animal. The blood on the mercy seat represented the price that had to be paid for the sins of the people. The price was an innocent life.

Q: This is getting confusing.

A: I know, but stay with me. More than three thousand years ago, when the ark was being used to store and transport the tablets, God used the language of ritual and symbol to communicate with his people. In the world they lived in, this would have been much easier to understand than it is for us today. Anyway, the innocent blood on the mercy seat, which sat on top of the ark, was positioned symbolically between God and his people. When God looked down at the ark, he in effect didn't see the Law that condemned the Israelites for failing to keep it. Instead of seeing the Law, God saw the innocent blood.

Q: I think I'm getting it...

A: The Law condemned the people, but the innocent blood on the mercy seat shielded God's people from condemnation. The sacrifice of the innocent animal had "paid the price" for the people's collective sins. So instead of judging the people for their sins, a holy God saw the innocent blood and was therefore merciful—hence the term *mercy seat.*

Q: But if God was holy, why did he fail to judge their unholiness?

A: In a sense, he didn't "see" their unholiness. Instead, he looked down and saw innocent blood shed as a sacrifice for them, in place of their own blood.

Q: And the same thing happens in the New Testament?

A: Something similar happens. In the Old Testament, God used the symbolism of innocent blood to shield his people from the judgment of the Law. In the New Testament, it's not an innocent animal that is sacrificed but Jesus. That's why Jesus is often referred to as the Lamb of God, or Agnus Dei, to use the Latin term. Today anyone who accepts Jesus is shielded from the all-consuming fire of God's holiness. Jesus' blood protects his children from the judgment of God. So when God looks at someone who has accepted Jesus and the sacrifice he made on the cross, God doesn't see that person's unholiness; he sees instead the innocent blood of his Son. And that makes it possible for that person to come into the presence of God. That's how we are protected from the fire of God's holiness. So, yes, God's wrath is a scary thing, but when you understand that he turned it on himself so we could come into his presence for eternity, you realize his love for us is what we should be talking about.

The problem of evil is not one that can be dealt with pharmacologically or in any other human way. Only God has the power to solve the problem of evil. It's absurd to look elsewhere for a solution to something so utterly beyond our abilities. In a way, it's not unlike dealing with a tsunami by drawing the shades.

4

Were We Planned, or Are We an Accident?

The Question of Origins; God vs. Blind Evolution; the Meaning of Life

One of the great books of the twentieth century is a little-known classic titled *Chance or the Dance?* In glorious prose, the author, Thomas Howard, explains the two fundamental ways that most of us see the world. He calls one way "chance" and the other "the dance."

By "chance" Howard is referring to the view of the world we might call modern secular humanism. According to that view, everything in the universe, including you and me, got here entirely by chance, which is to say, completely by accident. And so it follows that our lives have no meaning. According to the "chance" view of the world, the death of six million Jews in the Holocaust has no significance whatsoever. Nor does a parent's love for a child. Nothing has meaning; there is no God; and when we die, that's it.

But then there's the "dance." What Howard means by that is there is a God who made us and loves us and who has filled the entire universe with purpose and meaning. The particular blue color of the sky, the beauty of flowers and children—all are part of the larger meaning of the universe and point back to the Creator himself. Each of us has a purpose, and the movement of the stars and planets and the unfolding of all of history are part of an infinitely complex dance that is being orchestrated by the Creator.[1]

Chance or the dance? One of these views basically says that nothing has any meaning, while the other view says that everything has meaning. It's quite a stark choice.

Q: What's the bottom line on the evolution vs. creationism controversy?

A: That's kind of a big question. I'm not sure there is a bottom line.

Q: Let me be more specific. I used to hear a lot about creationism, but lately I keep reading about something called intelligent design.

A: Right. Intelligent design is the name of a movement that continues to be attacked by the scientific establishment as nonscience.

Q: That much I knew. But why the terminology of "intelligent design"?

A: It's the idea that the best available scientific evidence leads to the conclusion that life didn't evolve by chance but instead appears to have been designed by an intelligent being, or "designer." It's a position that says the universe is too complex to have developed through a series of random accidents and mutations, so there had to be an intelligent, organizing force behind it. Hence the term "intelligent design," which is called ID for short.

Q: I guess my real question is whether ID is something I should take seriously.

A: Without question. It has brought a whole new level of scrutiny and debate to the subject of evolution and has made a lot of people very uncomfortable, so it's worth taking seriously for those reasons alone. In fact, some of the claims of ID are so compelling it's surprising they didn't become widely known long ago.

Q: But isn't ID just a new way of referring to creationism?

A: Not at all. The efforts to bat it away by calling it creationism are mostly just a political tactic on the part of people who feel threatened by it. When people feel threatened, they often try to shut down the debate before it gets started, but this is a debate we should have. Ironically, the scientific establishment is doing something like what the church did with Galileo. But that's always the nature of power. Every movement, no matter what its original intentions, can get somehow corrupted. You see it with the church through the Middle Ages—and you see it now with parts of the scientific community. Some are afraid or angry or offended somehow, and they do everything they can to stifle dissent.

Q: Are you sure ID presents this much of a threat?

A: It certainly looks that way. A handful of ID theorists have some of the biggest proponents of Darwinian theory on the defensive. You can see how the leading evolutionists would be a little upset. They thought they were boxing a tomato can, but instead they've been knocked down a couple of times and are embarrassed and angry. To switch metaphors, it's something like watching Sir Francis Drake's smaller, faster boats outmaneuvering the ungainly galleons of the Spanish Armada. It's certainly entertaining. But it's also instructive.

Honestly, many of the people involved in the world of ID are serious scientists who are trying to account for the evidence they have observed. The evidence has led them to the conclusion that things could not have evolved to where they are today merely by accident.

Q: But why is this information just now coming to light after one hundred fifty years of Darwinism?

A: The more we study the universe—and of course we've been able to study it in greater detail and with better tools in recent years—the more we see evidence of deliberate design coming to light. Scientists today have evidence that wasn't available to Darwin, and there's more every day. The most recent evidence leads many to the conclusion that life on planet Earth didn't get here by chance, or what has been called "blind evolution."

Q: I assume you're not referring to evolution that has really weak eyesight.

A: Correct. Blind evolution is basically what Thomas Howard is talking about in his book *Chance or the Dance?* It's the idea that all life on the planet evolved completely by chance and without God or any intelligent force being involved in any way. The concept of God—or even some nameless intelligent force—being involved in the process is simply unacceptable to proponents of blind evolution. You could say you believe in the idea that life evolved over millions of years, but if you believed God was somehow behind the process, many scientists would still cry foul. They would argue that any possibility of a God being involved was inherently unscientific. That's a radical point of view, especially when there is so much evidence leading to the conclusion that there probably *was* an intelligent force involved. And it's ironic.

Q: Why ironic?

A: Proponents of blind evolution say that any mention of God or an intelligent creative force is unscientific, but how can it be unscientific if that's where the evidence is leading? To say "No, it can't lead there! Anywhere but *there*!" is to try to shut down the debate and to refuse to go where logic and the evidence are taking you. They are trying to preempt even the possibility that an "intelligent designer" could have been involved. They are saying that allowing the idea of God into the conversation is fundamentally unscientific.

Q: And you're saying it's not.

A: Absolutely. The idea that science and God are incompatible would be a shock to the greatest names science has produced, including Newton and Einstein, not to mention Darwin himself. The idea that the universe is knowable and worth exploring and understanding comes out of the idea that an intelligent being created it and gave it order. Science itself arose out of a world-view that includes God! That's the most ironic thing of all.

Q: If ID is based on science, then why does a large segment of the scientific community oppose it?

A: Good question. Science is supposed to be about reality and discovering the nature of reality, which means you don't dismiss anything out of hand. It's supposed to be committed to following the best evidence no matter where it leads. So if a closer examination of the universe suggests some manner of intelligent mind behind everything, then we need to figure out how to take that into account. We can't say we'll take everything into account *but that.*

No one is saying the intelligence behind the universe is a man in the clouds with a white beard. But the idea that there is some intelligent being seems to be more and more probable. Maybe in the past we could fool ourselves, before we knew what the inside of a cell looked like in detail. We could fool ourselves before we knew there wasn't any fossil evidence to "fill in the gaps." But now we've got to deal with the new facts and let them lead us wherever they will lead us.

Q: Can you give some examples of this new evidence?

A: The most famous example is the cell itself. Before the 1950s we didn't have microscopes powerful enough to really see what was going on inside cells, so it was easy to say that cells just got here via natural selection. But once technology progressed to the point that we could see what was going on inside a cell, it became clear that what was going on was so outrageously complicated that it would be highly improbable for it to have developed simply by chance.

It's something like this. Imagine a guy who is legally blind unless he wears his glasses, and then he loses his glasses. He can see well enough to get by, but just barely. One day on the beach he picks up something that feels like a thin stone. He puts it in his pocket and doesn't give it another thought. Later he finds his glasses and takes a look at what he thought was a stone. It's not a stone but a pocket watch. He removes the back of the watch and looks inside, and he can't believe the intricacy of its gears and levers. Instinctively, because he can now see details that he was blind to before, he realizes there had to be a designer involved. This was no shiny rock tossed up on the beach. This was made by an intelligent being.

We need to process all the new scientific findings, and

in this case when we do, we see more and more pocket watches and fewer and fewer stones.

Q: What else do we know today that we didn't know a few decades ago?

A: Well, one thing we know is that half of what we were taught in school about evolution was mistaken. Actually some of it was embarrassingly mistaken.

Q: Such as?

A: Remember the story of the black-and-white moths and how they changed their colors to avoid predators? They would supposedly blend in with the color of the tree bark they had landed on.

Q: It's starting to ring a bell.

A: Well, it turns out that the moths did not change colors after all.

Q: What about those photos in my textbook? I remember photos.

A: Most people remember those photos. But they were staged. The moths never landed on the trees. The moths were actually dead and were glued to the trees.

Q: And?

A: No one meant to deceive anyone in a malicious way, but millions of students got bad information.

Do you remember the phrase "ontogeny recapitulates phylogeny"?

Q: That's something I had to memorize for the midterm test. How could I forget it?

A: Well, don't get upset. But it's not true.

Q: But what about the drawings of the different embryos and how they were all similar?

A: Right, the famous embryo drawings that were in every biology textbook. The ones that showed that human embryos were just like frog and fish embryos. The ones that showed that humans have gills when we're in our mothers' wombs!

Q: Precisely!

A: There's just one problem.

Q: What's the problem?

A: We didn't have gills. Haeckel, who made those drawings, fudged them. They are simply not true. The gills are phony! Haeckel fudged the drawings based on what he wanted to believe and doubtless what he actually believed. But he was wrong. We don't have gills in the womb any more than we have wings and flipper feet and tails right now. It's just a terrible mistake that was perpetuated and sold to generations of school kids.[2]

Q: Next you'll be telling me Pluto isn't a planet.

A: It's not, but let's not get into that right now. We need to stick to biology.

Q: But those drawings were presented as established fact. I'm beginning to wonder what else I thought I knew that is now known to be false.

A: Don't take it too hard. We were just kids listening to our teachers, who were following the textbooks they were given.

Q: Are you about done with all this?

A: Just one more. Remember the pictures of how the horse evolved from the little prehistoric eohippus to the big, modern-day, Trigger-sized horse?

Q: Sure. I loved those little horse ancestors...

A: A lot of us did. But the whole concept of the horses evolving like that was, alas, made up. It's just not true.[3]

Q: Forgive me, but the salt-and-pepper moths, the embryo drawings, and the cute evolving horses were the pillars upon which my knowledge of evolution rested.

A: I'm sorry. But can you imagine how folks felt when they found out that the earth wasn't flat or that it wasn't the center of the universe? Accepting a new paradigm is never easy. Science marches on.

Q: I've heard backers of ID talking about something called "irreducible complexity." What is that?

A: Irreducible complexity means that something is so complex it can't be reduced into simpler parts. So it's irreducibly complex. It's the idea that an organism is too complicated to have evolved from something simpler.

Q: I need an example.

A: Think about your standard mousetrap. That's the example put forth by Michael Behe, one of the main proponents of the ID movement. He explains that a mousetrap is the sort of thing that couldn't have evolved from something simpler, because its five components all need to be there simultaneously for it to work. If you take away just one part, the whole thing ceases to function. It's irreducibly complex—you can't reduce it down to simpler components. Not that a mousetrap is a living organism, but the principle is the same. The mechanism makes no sense unless all five components are there together and put together in exactly the right way. We can't envision an earlier, simpler version of the mousetrap that was later improved upon. It's either the whole mousetrap exactly as we know it, or it's nothing.[4]

Q: So a mousetrap proves ID?

A: No, it's just a handy illustration. For examples that hit closer to home, take the human eye or the single cell. It doesn't seem to make logical sense that they evolved—not if you know anything about them and about how natural selection is supposed to work. The level of design of the eye or a single human cell is so extraordinary that it doesn't seem to make logical sense that they evolved from something less complicated.

Q: What do scientists who oppose this point of view say about it?

A: As of now, they refuse to accept the possibility of ID, so there's no real conversation. They feel certain that at some point we will better understand how these things evolved. You could say—again, not without irony—that they have faith in something and that the evidence won't move them.

We can argue whether evolution took place or exactly how it happened. That's a healthy conversation and one we shouldn't be afraid to have. It's exciting to think that the universe actually makes sense and that by using science, math, and logic we can understand it. But who created the beauty of the universe, and who gave it the layers and layers of order? Do the beauty and order of our world have meaning, or are they just an illusion of meaning? Is the very idea of meaning meaningless? Chance or the dance? That is the question.

5

How Can Anyone Know What Jesus Would Do?

Following Jesus Without Growing a Beard; How to Be Yourself; Jesus' Stance on Eating Meat

Most of us have heard the biblical story of David and Goliath. But we rarely hear about what happened *before* David went onto the battlefield. At the time, Saul was king over Israel, and Israel was at war with the Philistines. The Philistine warrior Goliath was challenging the Israelites to find one man to fight him. Battles were sometimes settled by a single fight between two men, but no one in King Saul's army dared go against the giant Goliath.

David's brothers were deployed with the Israelite army, and when David brought them some food from home, he was scandalized that no one would go up against Goliath. He decided to do it himself, knowing God would give him the strength to win.

When David asked King Saul's permission, Saul gave David armor to wear, including a coat of chain mail and a bronze helmet. But David had never worn such things before. He was a shepherd, and while protecting his flocks, David had gone up against lions and bears dressed as he was and armed only with a sling and a simple shepherd's staff. So he decided against the armor. He would go against the giant dressed as a shepherd, wielding a sling. Being himself and trusting in God had always worked before, and David figured they would probably work for him now.

Q: Every now and then I still see somebody wearing one of those WWJD bracelets. I know the letters stand for "What Would Jesus Do?" and on the one hand it's a good idea. But it also seems a bit ridiculous.

A: Why?

Q: How can anyone know what Jesus would do in a particular circumstance? He lived in another time and place. It's a different world today.

A: I see what you mean. But there are still many cases where we can know what he would do. We know he would always obey God's commandments. That's not something we need to think too hard about. But I understand what you mean; there are times when it's impossible to know exactly what decision Jesus would make if he were in our shoes. He is the ultimate model for human behavior, but what that means is more complicated than trying to figure out exactly what Jesus would do in a certain situation—like whether he would drive a car with a stick shift or an automatic, or whether he would prefer a vacation in the mountains or at the shore.

Q: Or whether he would drive sixty-four in a fifty-five-mph zone.

A: Right. That's a particularly tricky one, so let's skip it.

Q: Fine. But seriously, I've even wondered if doing what Jesus would do means I'd have to talk about God all the time—and stay single. I'm not trying to be funny. Where do you draw the line?

A: That's a great question, but look at it this way. God created every one of us to be ourselves. There is no doubt that God wants us to emulate Jesus, but ultimately what God wants is for each of us to be ourselves—not in the cheesy sense of "I gotta be me" but in the deepest and truest sense of what it means to be who you are.

Q: I'm not sure I'm following you.

A: It's like this: The more we are ourselves, the more we are like Jesus. And the more we are like Jesus, the more we are ourselves.

Q: Now you've lost me completely.

A: Here's the thing: Jesus was the only person in history who was totally and completely himself at all times. He fully lived out his mission and perfectly carried out his Father's will. So being like Jesus ultimately means being yourself as you follow God, just as Jesus was himself as he fulfilled God's will on earth.

Q: Of course he was himself. Who else would he be? How can people not be themselves?

A: Well, think about how often you hear people say, "Just be yourself." Especially when someone is about to attempt something that makes them nervous, such as public speaking or going on a blind date. That person's friends often say, "Just be yourself."

If it's such an easy thing to do, why are people always having to tell others to do it? Your friends give you this advice because being yourself isn't something you automatically do when you're worried about what others will think of you. But not being yourself doesn't happen only when you're in a tense situation. Most of us are afraid to be who we are even in normal, everyday situations. On some level we are all pretending to be something or someone we're not. Even if we're not really aware of it, and even if it's just temporary.

Q: I think I'm following...

A: And who can even say they know who they really are? We're somehow always trying to figure that out. Except for Jesus.

Q: Why is that?

A: Jesus knew *exactly* who he was—and he was never anything other than exactly who he was. But what that really means is that he knew exactly what his purpose was on earth. He never strayed from that, the way we do.

Q: But why is it so hard for us to live out our purpose on earth?

A: Because of the Fall—the first sin that was committed against God by the first humans. To use a theological term, every human is "fallen." We all fell from grace and are in need of God's redemption. That's why we need a Savior. Jesus was without sin, and he came to restore us to where we were before we fell from grace. That's why he is sometimes referred to as the "last Adam."[1] He came to restore humanity to its original condition, so to speak—to who we *really* are and to who we were meant to be all along. And Jesus himself is a picture of restored humanity, the state that Adam and Eve were in before sin entered the world.

Q: Because Jesus was perfect, he can show us how to be ourselves?

A: Yes. Jesus is a living picture of human life as it was meant to be lived, in perfect communion with God. There wasn't any part of Jesus that was broken, selfish, or outside God's will. He was precisely as he was meant to be; he was totally himself. And he holds out hope that we, too, can become who we are supposed to be: ourselves.

Q: But why do people have to be obedient to God to be themselves?

A: First, because we're not in the same condition we were when God created us. Before the Fall, humans had an unbroken, completely open relationship with God. But that relationship was ruptured by sin. Jesus made it possible for the relationship to be reconciled so that we can be restored to our original condition, so to speak.

Q: So being unbroken is part of being ourselves?

A: Yes! When we find Jesus and allow him to heal our broken relationship with God, we are suddenly able to learn who we really are. We can only discover who we are through a relationship with the one who created us. Only through him can we find our true identity. In discovering Jesus, we discover ourselves.

Q: I've never heard it put that way before.

A: Not being able to truly be ourselves is the human condition. As I said, people are afraid that others won't like them if they're just being themselves. We pretend we have more money than we do to impress certain people. We pretend to be more important than we really are. We create a kind of role for ourselves, something that might be just a little off of who we really are, or it might be a big phony act—and anyone who really knows us sees it as an act. Perhaps we've been putting on the act for so long that we hardly know it's an act anymore; we think that's who we actually are. Perhaps we're trying to be who our parents think we should be or who our friends think we should be. But we have no idea who we really are. We need to find out who we are in God's eyes, who he made us to be from the very beginning.

God created us, and he wants to tell us who we really are. But that can't happen unless we have a relationship with him. We have to learn how to hear his voice, even if it's just in subtle ways. And we have to know how to let him lead us in the direction he has prepared for us. And that, of course, is precisely how Jesus lived his life.

Q: So doing what Jesus would do doesn't mean I have to become a rabbi or remain single?

A: Exactly. God didn't intend for every human being to be a religious teacher or to live in Palestine. But every one of us needs to be connected to God in the way that Jesus was so we can know who we are supposed to be. God doesn't tell us who we are and then leave us to struggle on our own. He stays beside us in the midst of it, just as he was with Jesus.

The main thing about being like Jesus and living as he did means having a close relationship with our heavenly Father. All the details will follow. So when someone asks what Jesus would do, they need to know that following him doesn't necessarily mean walking down dusty roads and talking about the kingdom of God. It means having the kind of relationship with the one who made you that is so real you are able to begin being who he made you to be.

Q: The beard and sandals are optional, then?

A: Right. Unless that's who God made you to be, of course. And to be perfectly accurate, God didn't make us.

Q: What?

A: Well, he did make us, but that's not the complete story. Actually, he *invented* us. Most of us can make a sandwich, but we didn't invent the idea of a sandwich. That's a whole other level of creating something. And God invented each of us. He came up with the idea of you and me. So he knows us more intimately than anyone else ever could, including ourselves, and he alone knows who we truly were meant to be. He is longing to share that with us and help us get there.

Q: Can I ask a follow-up question?

A: Why not?

Q: Okay, what would Jesus eat?

A: Well, that depends. What's on the menu?

Q: Let me be more specific. Would Jesus eat meat? Doesn't the Bible say "Thou shalt not kill," and isn't it true that there was no meat eating in the Garden of Eden?

A: Well, yes. But there's more to it. The commandment that prohibits killing isn't referring to animals. In fact, a more accurate translation of that commandment is "You shall not murder."[2] The commandment refers to human beings.

Q: So we can kill animals whenever we feel like it?

A: Of course not. The Bible makes it very clear that the taking of any life—including animals—is a serious thing. So whenever anyone kills animals for any reason, including for food, it's a serious issue. But the Bible makes it clear that it's permissible to kill animals and to eat meat.

Q: I don't recall reading that Adam and Eve threw any barbecues.

A: Well, it's true that in the beginning there was no meat eating, but after the Flood everything changed, and God made animals available for—among other things—sustenance. But you're right, there seems to be some sense that this isn't the way it was originally meant to be.

Q: But doesn't it make sense that God would want us to live according to the way it was before sin entered the Garden of Eden?

A: Perhaps, but Jesus, who was sinless, ate meat. If God in human form ate meat, it's hard to see how it can be wrong for us.

Q: When did Jesus eat meat? Was there a miracle of the loaves and the meat knishes that I missed?

A: We know that Jesus was an observant Jew, so we know, for example, that he never ate a cheeseburger. That wouldn't have been kosher. But we also know that all observant Jews ate lamb at Passover. They were commanded to do so by God. So there you have an instance where we know that Jesus ate meat.

Q: But that's just one instance.

A: It's an annual instance. We know that Jesus ate meat at the Passover meal about thirty times in his life. And of course he multiplied the loaves of bread and the few fish donated by a young boy when a crowd of thousands needed to be fed. So he obviously didn't have a problem with people eating fish. In the gospel of John, Jesus even cooks a breakfast of fish for the disciples.[3]

Q: So he cooked fish, but did Jesus ever eat fish himself? Some people will cook things but not eat them.

A: Yes, Jesus ate fish. Probably many times. But the one instance we have in the Scriptures where he is actually eating it is right after the resurrection. The first thing Jesus does when he appears to the disciples is to ask for something to eat, and the disciples give him a piece of broiled fish and a honeycomb.[4] And not only does that show Jesus eating fish, but it proves that after he rose from the dead, he wasn't a disembodied spirit. He was still a flesh-and-blood human being.

Q: Jesus ate broiled fish?

A: Yes.

Q: Were any particular herbs and spices mentioned?

A: I'm not sure, but I'll look into it. In the meantime, try Old Bay. It works on everything.

David the shepherd boy understood that it was God who had given him his earlier victories against lions and bears. He would trust God to give him victory against Goliath. The story of David's passing up Saul's offer of armor has something to do with the idea that we need to know who we are—we need to be ourselves. But it's also important to realize that we can't really and truly be ourselves if we're not depending on God.

6

What Does the Bible Say About Abortion?

Why the Bible Doesn't Mention Abortion; Religion and Public Policy

Two centuries ago a diminutive politician named William Wilberforce tried to bring his religious views on certain subjects into British society. In most circles such a thing was considered gauche at best, and Wilberforce was deeply hated by many. Among those who vilified him was a certain Lord Melbourne, whose complaint has become famous in its own right: "Things are coming to a pretty pass," Melbourne said, "when religion is allowed to invade private life!"[1]

But Wilberforce would not be dissuaded, and twenty years after he began his exceedingly unpopular crusade for abolition, he finally succeeded. In 1807 it became illegal to buy or sell human beings anywhere in the British Empire.

Q: What exactly does the Bible say about abortion?

A: The Bible doesn't mention abortion.

Q: Are you kidding?

A: Would I kid about something like that? But I can see where you might get the idea that the Bible is big on condemning abortion.

Q: I could have sworn it was in there...

A: You probably got the idea from noticing that most of the people who speak out against abortion often quote the Bible.

Q: Then I'm not dreaming.

A: Of course not. But just because the Bible doesn't specifically mention abortion doesn't mean it doesn't set forth some very clear ideas on the subject. It does.

Q: But without mentioning abortion specifically?

A: Right. The Bible doesn't mention a lot of things specifically, but you can still get a very clear idea where it stands on these subjects. For example, the Bible doesn't specifically prohibit cheating on one's taxes or making fake IDs or copying someone's answers when you take the SAT. But when you read the Bible, you get the general idea that none of these is recommended. It also doesn't mention pole-vaulting at the opera or putting brussels sprouts into the collection plate at church.

Q: But how am I supposed to know what God thinks about something if it's not specifically mentioned?

A: You have to use your noodle, pal. Boot up the hard drive, as it were.

Q: Doesn't it just become a guessing game at that point?

A: Not at all. The idea that we can find a specific text in the Bible on every topic is bad theology. It's nice when there is a verse that makes everything crystal clear, but generally speaking, the Bible was never intended to be a reference book that spells everything out. It would be awfully convenient if it had bullet points on every subject, but it doesn't. And since God inspired every word of it, we have to assume that he didn't want it to be that kind of book.

Q: So how do we find what it says on a subject such as abortion?

A: We look at the larger context and at broader themes and principles. From that we can extrapolate rather clearly what God thinks on a large number of issues, even if they aren't mentioned specifically. We can also look to Christian tradition. For two thousand years the church has been interpreting the Bible, and we need to look to that tradition for guidance.

Q: But the church sometimes changes how it interprets certain teachings. Aren't we supposed to read the Bible for ourselves rather than just accept what other people say about it?

A: We need a balance. All kinds of folks claim to find all kinds of things in the Bible that simply aren't there. People have used verses of Scripture to justify everything from slavery to polygamy. There are plenty of examples of people using the Bible to legitimize their own preferences. We all need help in reading and interpreting Scripture so we don't go off the rails. But this is a separate issue. We were talking about abortion, no?

Q: Yes, but I still don't see how we are supposed to know what the Bible says if it doesn't say it.

A: Here's an analogy. The U.S. Constitution doesn't specifically prohibit drunk driving, but that doesn't mean drunk driving is constitutional, does it?

Q: I don't think so.

A: Cars didn't exist in the 1780s, so the framers didn't include language regarding drunk driving. But there's enough in the Constitution to help us figure out how to apply its principles to situations that the men who wrote it never could have anticipated.

In the same way, we interpret what Scripture has to say on various issues based on its broader principles. And just because some folks twist what the Bible says to make it serve their own purposes doesn't mean the truth itself is changeable. Either God defines what truth is, or he doesn't. And if we want to find the truth, we have to be willing to accept the Bible on its own terms and not limit it just to what we're comfortable with. Because God loves us, we can trust him, and we can rely on what the Bible says. God's opinion on the matter is in our best interest, and it's more than an opinion. It's eternal truth, and it's full of hope and love and joy, and we can trust it.

Q: I can understand the Constitution not mentioning drunk driving because there were no cars in the 1780s, but are you saying there were no abortions when the Bible was written?

A: Strangely enough, that's almost the case, yes. Life and children were so revered in ancient Hebrew culture that the idea of abortion was almost unthinkable then.

Q: But if the Bible doesn't mention the subject, how do people get the idea that it's against abortion?

A: There are several passages that serve as a starting point. First of all, the Bible clearly says that taking human life is wrong, so the real question is whether the Bible considers a fetus to be a human life. If it does, then obviously it would follow that abortion is prohibited because it involves taking a human life.

Q: Okay, I'm with you.

A: And to figure that out, the first verses I'd look at are in Psalms. In Psalms, David wrote that God "knit me together in my mother's womb."[2] He also says God knew him, even when his body was "unformed,"[3] and that he is "fearfully and wonderfully made."[4] So it seems pretty obvious the Bible regards David as a human being even before he was born. Then in the book of Exodus, a passage states that if a man injures a pregnant woman and causes her to give birth prematurely, there are required penalties. If the baby survives without serious injury, the man is fined. But if the baby dies, the man gets the death penalty.[5]

And finally, in the book of Jeremiah, God is speaking to Jeremiah and says, "Before I formed you in the womb I knew you, before you were born…I appointed you as a prophet to the nations."[6] These verses make it clear that a fetus in the womb really is regarded as a human life.

And in the New Testament, there is a beautiful image in the gospel of Luke where John the Baptist leaps in his mother's womb.[7]

Q: I don't remember that.

A: Mary had just become pregnant with Jesus, and she went to visit her cousin Elizabeth. Elizabeth was six months pregnant at the time with the baby who would grow up to become John the Baptist.

Q: Jesus and John the Baptist were cousins?

A: Yes! That alone is worth talking about for a while. But the Bible tells us that in the moment Mary greeted her cousin, the baby in Elizabeth's womb "leaped." Elizabeth was immediately "filled with the Holy Spirit," and God spoke through her. She said to Mary, "Blessed are you among women, and blessed is the child you will bear!"[8] It's an extraordinary moment, to say the least.

Here is a picture of two women and two unborn

babies, one six months along and the other probably not much more than what we would today call a zygote or a blastocyst or at best an embryo. But the Bible makes it pretty clear that God calls it a human being already. The unborn John wasn't leaping at the *possibility* of human life but at human life itself.

Q: Interesting.

A: This doesn't mean that everyone has to agree with what the Bible says about unborn human life, but if someone wants to know what it says, that's what it says. And although the Bible says there is a penalty for the taking of a human life, whether born or unborn, it also says a person can find total forgiveness and healing through Jesus Christ. That often gets lost in the noisy debate over abortion. No woman should ever feel that God is condemning her if she has had an abortion. We all do things that call for forgiveness and healing, and that essentially is the central teaching of the Bible—not what is or isn't right, but that there is hope and healing and forgiveness for all of us who have made mistakes, whether large or small.

Q: So why do you think the abortion debate is so rancorous?

A: Many reasons. Part of the problem is that this issue has turned into a political battle, and in politics the idea of treating your opponents with love is usually forgotten even by so-called Christians. If one's larger goal is to win a political battle, then Jesus' command to love your enemies can seem annoyingly quaint and unrealistic. People who are really passionate about this issue can get so focused on winning that they lose sight of the most important thing—obeying Jesus in their own lives and loving their enemies. Loving your enemies is much, much harder than screaming at them. But if opponents of abortion say it's wrong because God says it is, then they also have to say that hating their enemies is wrong because God says it is.

Q: Wouldn't it just be better if people of faith stayed out of the dirty world of politics?

A: Not at all. Christians are supposed to be salt and light in every part of their culture, from the world of entertainment to the world of politics. But if God calls us to enter those fields, we have to behave the way he wants us to behave. We're not there just to win but to bring God's love and grace and forgiveness and kindness—even and especially for our opponents and enemies—into that process. That's the most difficult battle and probably the most important.

Q: Thinking about moral issues that have become political footballs brings up another issue—the constitutional question of the separation of church and state.

A: You're right; this is a huge issue. But the Constitution doesn't mention the separation of church and state.

Q: Now cut that out.

A: I'm not kidding.

Q: First you tell me the Bible doesn't mention abortion. Now you claim the Constitution doesn't mention the separation of church and state. I feel like I've landed in an episode of The Twilight Zone. You're not an alien, are you? or a giant insect?

A: No. At least I hope I'm not. But believe me, the Constitution really doesn't use the phrase "separation of church and state."

Q: Then where do we get the phrase?

A: We get it from a letter written by Thomas Jefferson. The *concept* of the separation of church and state is found in the Constitution, but the phrase itself is not there. Jefferson referred to a "wall of separation between church and state" in a letter written to a group of Baptists in Danbury, Connecticut—which I'm proud to say is my hometown. *Go, Hatters!*

Q: Hatters?

A: Yes, Hatters. Anyway, Jefferson wrote the letter in 1801, several years *after* the Constitution was ratified.

Q: So you're saying the separation of church and state is not constitutional?

A: Not at all. As I say, the concept of the separation of church and state is entirely constitutional. The letter written to the

Danbury Baptists simply gives us a picture of Jefferson's further thinking on the concept, which is captured in the Constitution's establishment clause.

Q: And that is...?

A: The Constitution says the government can "make no law respecting an establishment of religion, or prohibiting the free exercise thereof."[9] That's what Jefferson is referring to. Let me quote his letter. I have it here someplace.

Q: Jefferson's letter?

A: It's probably not the original. Anyway, these are his exact words:

> Believing with you that religion is a matter which lies solely between man & his god, that he owes account to none other for his faith or his worship, that the legitimate powers of government reach actions only, and not opinions, I contemplate with sovereign reverence that act of the whole American people which declared that *their* legislature should make no law respecting an establishment of religion, or prohibiting the free exercise thereof, thus building a wall of separation between church and state.... Adhering to this expression of the supreme will of the nation in behalf of the rights of conscience, I shall see with sincere satisfaction the progress of those sentiments which tend to restore to man all his natural rights, convinced he has no natural right in opposition to his social duties.[10]

Q: So what does "separation of church and state" mean?

A: There's an amazing amount of misunderstanding about it. Many people have gotten the idea that it means religion has no place in public life, which is entirely wrong. All the Founding Fathers assumed religion and faith would play a big role in the life of the country they were founding. And not only did they assume it, they welcomed it—in fact, most of them saw it as utterly vital to the American Experiment. John Adams said our Constitution "is designed only for a moral and religious people. It is wholly inadequate for any other."[11]

Ironically, the concept of the separation of church and state has nothing to do with people of faith threatening to take over government; it has to do with precisely the opposite threat—government taking over the church. If you can believe it, the idea behind Jefferson's "wall of separation" was that religion—and various Christian denominations—needed to be protected from the government. All through history governments have taken over churches and dictated what people could and couldn't believe. But in America, the idea was that this wouldn't happen. People of faith would be free to worship as they pleased, without government interference and control.

Q: This is not what I've heard on the subject. You're sure?

A: Absolutely. But based on the way this issue is usually treated in the news media, you'd never know the Constitution was protecting religion from the government and not the other way around. The concept of the establishment clause was to make sure that all faiths and denominations would be treated equally. In England, there was a state church, which was favored over other denominations. The same was true in Greece with the Greek Orthodox Church and in Italy with the Roman Catholic Church and in so many other countries, then and today. But in the United States, because of the establishment clause, we can't have a state church. For us, religion and government are officially separate. But as I say, the separation of church and state isn't meant to keep the churches out of government but to keep government out of the churches.

When the British slave trade suddenly ended in 1807, it prompted other nations to follow suit. Within a few decades the slave trades of all other major nations ceased forever, and eventually slavery itself was abolished in those same countries. Perhaps better than anyone before or since, William Wilberforce understood the proper role of faith in politics, and for that the whole world is in his debt.

7

Does God Want People to Be Rich?

Long-Term Wealth; Money and Goodness; the Bible and Money

In 1963 the Beatles recorded a song called "Money." You probably remember the opening lines:

> The best things in life are free.
> But you can give them to the birds and bees.[1]

We all agree with the first line, of course. We know it's true. But we've heard it so often that it's become a cliché. The second line of the song is a sharp, funny departure from the first, expressing what so many of us have thought at one time or another, particularly when someone cloyingly tells us that the best things in life are free!

As the song continues, the singer makes explicit what we already know he feels, telling us in no uncertain terms that it's money he wants! It's a good song because we all recognize ourselves in it. While we know what's really and truly valuable, we also know that living in this world is extraordinarily difficult when money is a problem, and for most of us it usually is. No matter how much we know that money isn't the solution to our problems, we simply can't pretend that we're above having to deal with it, either. So what's the answer?

Q: Does God want us to get rich?

A: Yes.

Q: Yes?

A: And no.

Q: Yes and no? Could you be a little more specific?

A: There's no short, easy answer to this. To really and truly understand God's perspective on this subject, and on almost all subjects, it helps to think of him as the ultimate loving Parent.

Q: Okay.

A: If we think about the best parent imaginable, we can usually understand that God loves us more than we can comprehend and wants the very best for us.

Q: So then he wants us to be happy, which includes being wealthy!

A: Yes, but God doesn't have a shallow view of what wealth is. Like the best parent imaginable, God is wise. And in God's case, he's *infinitely* wise. He knows that sometimes simply giving us things can spoil us instead of bless us—that they could actually hurt us in the long run. And if a really great earthly parent has the long term in mind, God has the *longest* term in mind.

Q: What's the "longest term"?

A: Eternity. Just as a human parent wants children to thrive over the long haul, God wants us all to thrive over the longest haul there is. He doesn't want us to have wealth just in the here and now; he wants us to have eternal wealth. A parent chooses not to always give his or her children what they want when they want it, such as feeding them candy and ice cream at every meal, because the parent knows that would harm the child in the future. In the same way, God refuses to give us everything we want when we want it because he knows that could harm us eternally. And he really wants us to have as much eternal wealth as possible.

Q: What do you mean by "eternal wealth"? I'm guessing it doesn't include a red Ferrari...

A: That's a safe bet. God has a far grander and longer-range view of wealth than wanting to give us the occasional sports car. That doesn't mean God opposes money and wealth. He knows money can alleviate suffering and do a lot of good, and he knows poverty can mean suffering and misery. But God also knows better than anyone that money can't buy happiness. He sees both sides of the issue, and ultimately he wants *us* to see both sides. Possessing wisdom is far more valuable than having financial wealth, so, yes, if there is a choice, God would certainly rather have us poor and wise than rich and foolish. And that's because he wants us to have real wealth so we will enjoy a richness of life that goes beyond our bank accounts.

Q: So you're really saying that God <u>doesn't</u> want us to be rich.

A: I'm not saying that at all. No loving parent wants his child to be poor, but let's face it, there are worse things than being poor.

Q: Okay, what's worse than being poor?

A: Well, how about having everything you could ever want and turning into an insensitive, narcissistic, grotesquely spoiled human being who uses and abuses other people in order to get his own way?

Q: Unfortunately, I know some people like that, and, yes, that would be pretty bad. Got it.

A: God cares about us so much that he goes out of his way to help us rely on him and not on ourselves, our skills, our intelligence, or our wealth. He wants us to love him and trust him and end up in his presence for eternity. And for some of us, that process might include God's allowing us to be poor or at least not as wealthy as we might like.

Q: So it's a choice between having money or going to heaven?

A: Of course not! It's not a matter of either-or, and it's not primarily about money. It's about what you trust—whom you make your god. Jesus said it's easier for a camel to go through the eye of a needle than for a rich man to enter heaven.[2] That's scary, if you think about it. And if Jesus said it, we should think about it and think hard.

Q: So money is dangerous to our souls?

A: Absolutely. But again, that doesn't mean God is against money. Nor should we be against it. No one wants to be poor or to struggle financially, but we also know that money is not the ultimate answer to our struggles. If we turn to God in our difficulties, the toughest times in life can end up being the best times in life. Our struggles can become times when we learn the most and change the most. We can and should become wiser through our sufferings.

Of course we don't seek out suffering—that would be foolish. And we don't seek out financial difficulty, but sometimes while we are in the midst of financial difficulty, we learn things we never would have learned otherwise.

Q: Such as?

A: Such as compassion for others who are struggling, compassion for the poor. Have you ever noticed that wealthy people can be indifferent to financial struggles—unless they have gone through similar struggles themselves? Or that people who are successful sometimes act as though they have all the answers, which can be incredibly hurtful to someone who is suffering? It's a temptation to think those who are suffering or who are poor are either lazy or that they are getting what they deserve because they haven't done the right things in life.

Q: I've noticed that.

A: If God is concerned with a person's character and soul—if the real wealth that God wants us to have is eternal wealth, meaning he wants us to become more and more like him—then God wants us to be less self-centered and arrogant and more loving and humble. Getting us to that place in life is the most important kind of wealth God could give us.

Who can put a price on wisdom and humility and kindness and compassion? The Bible says wisdom is better than gold.[3] In a way, wisdom is the kind of money you can take with you to heaven, which means it's God's idea of real wealth, wealth you can never lose. But God wants us to understand that it's *real.* We should be motivated to do whatever it takes to get it, because we really and truly will be thrilled when we get to heaven. That's not a pie-in-the-sky idea.

Q: I understand, but just to be clear, you're not saying a wise person can't own a Maserati? I mean, what's so especially wise about driving a rusty AMC Pacer?

A: Of course, it's possible to be both rich and wise. King Solomon of Israel was known to be one of the wisest men who ever lived and was also one of the richest. But let's be honest. The odds are stacked against this combination. As we mentioned earlier, Jesus said it's easier for a camel to go through the eye of a needle than for a rich man to enter heaven. He was warning us that earthly riches can shape our thinking—that they *will* shape our thinking. We have to be very wary of that. Any good thing can be dangerous, because it can compete against God for our loyalty and affection. That's why Jesus said you can't serve God and mammon both.[4] By "mammon" he meant money. We have to choose who and what will get our allegiance.

Q: But what if a person is already rich? Is he supposed to get rid of his money?

A: It depends. There is nothing inherently wrong with being rich, just as there's nothing wrong with being beautiful or intelligent or athletic. These are all good things, and God wants the best for his children. The question is, what do we do with the good things—the gifts God has given us? God wants us to use everything he has given us for his purposes, not our own. God blesses us with gifts so we can be a blessing to others. Period. The only reason God allows some people to have money is so they can use it to bless others. And he will judge us on how we use what we've been given. God will judge us on how we spent every penny, especially if we have a lot of money.

Q: So you <u>are</u> saying that wealthy people should give away their money.

A: Not in a "redistribute the wealth" sense. But, yes, God does command us to be generous. Some people twist the words of Jesus to make it seem that he was some kind of proto-communist who advocated giving everything away. He didn't necessarily say that, but he did say we should use whatever we have to bless others, and that includes our money, our health, our abilities and talents, and any other resources we have. You could say we are supposed to transfer our wealth to heaven.[5]

Q: How are we supposed to transfer funds to heaven?

A: It's complicated. You have to fill out a special form, and you need two forms of ID.

Q: Ha. Seriously, what do you mean by "transferring wealth to heaven"?

A: Jesus said, "Do not store up for yourselves treasures on earth, where moth and rust destroy, and where thieves break in and steal. But store up for yourselves treasures in heaven."[6] He was talking about eternal riches, as we discussed earlier. Jesus makes it pretty clear that when we do God's will on earth we are accumulating "treasures in heaven." When you use your money to do something for God, it has eternal consequences, and you are accumulating eternal treasure.

There's a reason God tells some people to give away all they have to the poor, and there's a reason that Christians have always been encouraged to give away much of what they have to others. The reason is that it's good for the soul.

It reminds us that the money we have isn't really ours. God lends it to us, and we're to use it for his purposes, not ours.

Q: So God wants us to have less money? He wants us to suffer?

A: No, not ultimately. Not any more than a loving human parent wants her kids to suffer. But parents do want their children to learn and grow, and part of that process involves going through some difficulties, which can be painful. We want our children to grow, so we allow them to struggle with homework and chores and sports, because it's good for them. We don't want to hand them success on a platter. We know they won't enjoy it as much, and we want them to enjoy what they have as much as possible.

Q: And, I assume from what you're saying, that God wants us to endure difficulties for the same reasons.

A: It sure looks that way. He loves us more than we can imagine and wants us to enjoy the richness of life. But how we get there is another story. Anyone who says the Bible claims we are to have all the good things of life immediately doesn't understand the totality of who God really is. God is not some sugar daddy who dispenses gifts and spoils us; he's an infinitely loving Father who truly wants the best for us, in the very deepest sense.

Q: But what about the television preachers who say we should expect to enjoy financial abundance right now?

A: There is a grain of truth to that, but usually they turn the words of God into a simplistic formula for success and de-emphasize the larger truths of Scripture—and sometimes to serve their own ends, as when they constantly ask their viewers to send them money.

The money question, as I said at the start, is not an easy one to answer. There is nothing wrong with asking God for financial blessings, any more than it would be wrong to ask him to heal you if you were sick or to comfort you if you were suffering. But you have to be careful about telling God *how* he should bless you. God has all riches in store for his children in heaven that are more glorious and more real than any riches we can imagine in this life, so whether I get a Ferrari while I'm on earth may be a little beside the point.

Q: Doesn't the Bible say money is the root of all evil?

A: No. The Bible does not say money is the root of all evil.

Q: I could have sworn I'd heard that.

A: The Bible says the *love* of money is the root of evil. Actually, to be precise, it says the love of money is "a root of all kinds of evil."[7] That's a pretty big difference, really.

Q: But what about the money changers in the temple? Didn't Jesus rebuke them and knock over their tables?

A: Of course. But Jesus was dealing with a specific situation in which vendors were taking advantage of people who were coming to offer sacrifices at the temple. He was angry that the vendors had turned a holy place of worship into a marketplace, into a place where the focus was not on God but on commerce.[8]

Think about this: if money itself were the root of evil, would God tell us to give it to the poor? How can something that we give to others in order to bless them be anything but good?

Q: Speaking of helping the poor, doesn't the Bible say "God helps those who help themselves"?

A: Nope. The Bible doesn't make that statement any more than it says "money is the root of all evil." It's amazing how some things are repeated so much that eventually everyone believes they're true. "God helps those who help themselves" is actually from *Aesop's Fables.*

Q: Really?

A: Yep. One of the fables is titled "Hercules and the Wagoner." It's about a man whose wagon has gotten stuck in the mud, so he prays to one of the gods to help him. Actually he prays to Hercules, who by then had been promoted to demigod or something. Of course, Hercules appears and tells the man to put his shoulder to the wheel—literally—to help himself instead of just praying. That's where we get the phrase "put your shoulder to the wheel," of course. The moral tacked on at the end of the story is "The gods help those that help themselves."[9] That's where it originated, although we changed it to "God helps those who help themselves." It's not necessarily bad advice, but it's not exactly in the Bible.

Q: Live and learn.

A: We have to be careful about what we assume is in the Bible. There are a lot of confused ideas about God out there.

Q: But what about the idea that God helps those who help themselves? You said it's not entirely a bad idea.

A: There is some truth to it. God doesn't want us to sit around and wait for him to do everything for us. On the other hand, he doesn't want us to get ahead of him, either.

Q: How do you mean?

A: Many people who say "God helps those who help themselves" use it as an excuse to ignore God. They want to do everything on their own, the way they think it should be done. For example, if someone suggests to a friend that perhaps he should pray for guidance or ask God for help, the friend might shoot back, "Well, doesn't the Bible say God helps those who help themselves?" The bigger issue is that God wants us to admit our need and our weakness and acknowledge the fact that ultimately we rely on him for everything. God wants people to turn to him for guidance and help.

Q: So which is it? Do we go ahead and get things done, or do we wait around for God to help us?

A: We do both. We work best when we include God in whatever we are doing. That makes some of us uncomfortable, because it's often a lot more convenient to exclude God from some parts of our lives. It's easy to adopt the attitude that says "that is God's department, and this other part of my life is my department." But God says it's *all* his department. He wants us to be in a relationship with him that is based on trust, where we don't try to hide anything from him. We are meant to open every part of our lives to him and to know that we can totally trust him.

If you fear the implications of opening your whole life to God, then you don't really understand who God is. You don't understand how much he loves you, and you don't really believe that you can trust him completely.

Q: But you did say there is some merit to the statement that God helps those who go ahead and take action. Right?

A: Yes, God never tells us to sit and do nothing as we wait for him to come along and take care of things. Saint Paul wrote that Christians are expected to work if they are able, and they shouldn't be a burden to others if they can help it.[10] It's important to have a balanced attitude about this. We need to have a good sense of when God wants to do something for us and when he wants us to do something for ourselves. I've found that most of the time the problem is folks doing things on their own and then expecting God to get on board and make everything turn out right. But if you're keeping him out of the equation on the front end, he won't necessarily come along later and turn all your efforts into successes.

Jesus famously said we are to "render therefore unto Caesar the things which are Caesar's; and unto God the things that are God's."[11] Everyone has to deal with the reality and the necessity of money. We are required to pay our taxes and balance our checkbooks. But Jesus helps us see that there is another reality, somehow even more real than what's in our wallets. Deep within we realize that as useful as money is, the very best things really are free.

8

Why Would God Oppose Homosexuality?

God's Invention of Sex; How to Have Sex; Why We're Obsessed with Sex

Several years ago in the town of Laramie, Wyoming, a young man named Matt Shepard met two other men in a bar. Before the night was over, the two men brutally beat Shepard, tied him to a fence, and left him to die in a grisly tableau that shocked the nation. The news coverage seemed to offer only one response to the tragedy: either celebrate Shepard's homosexuality or, by default, condone the actions of the monsters who murdered him.

In past generations those who struggled with their sexuality were told to be silent and invisible, that there was no legitimate place where they could discuss their feelings. Today, many who hold to biblical teachings on sexuality are being told there is no legitimate forum for discussing the moral questions associated with homosexuality. One can't help but wonder what might have happened if the tragic death of Matt Shepard had instead opened up a genuine conversation on this profoundly important and difficult subject.

Q: I've heard that the Old Testament condemns sex acts between members of the same sex, but Jesus never mentions the subject. Since he didn't bother to condemn homosexuality, isn't it entirely possible he had no particularly strong feelings on the issue?

A: There are many things Jesus never mentioned, but assuming he endorsed something simply because he didn't explicitly mention it doesn't make sense. Jesus never talked about racism or spousal abuse, but can we seriously believe he condoned them?

Q: Okay, fair enough...

A: This is a lot like that other super-hot-button topic, abortion, because one of the main reasons we can have such a hard time understanding what the Bible teaches about it—even when we approach it with the very best intentions—is that we cannot rely on a few verses of isolated scripture. In order to really understand the biblical view of homosexuality, we have to take into account the Bible's view of sexuality in general. We need to get some context. Besides, let's face it, the subject is far too important to too may people to deal with in sound bites and clichés.

Q: Too true.

A: To begin with, the Bible leaves little doubt that God created sex specifically to be enjoyed in the lifelong commitment of a marriage between a man and a woman. So whenever two people engage in sex outside of that context, it's almost a non sequitur. In a funny way, it's not really sex at all, because in God's eyes sex is something that can't legitimately be separated from marriage. The two are parts of a single thing.

Q: You're saying that sex outside of marriage isn't actually sex?

A: In a way, yes. It's something like looking at every word in a book written in a language you don't understand. Is that really reading? Or like eating a wonderful meal and then, as bulimics do, getting rid of it—pardon the image. Is that really eating? It's hard to say what you'd call these activities. So sex outside of marriage may be physically gratifying, but that's not nearly the same as sex that is gratifying to both body and soul. God created sex and marriage to be something transcendent, a living image of God's union with his bride, the church. It's the holiest expression of a lifelong commitment between a man and a woman who are joined in marriage on the deepest and most intimate level possible. And from that holy union comes human life. God's two creatures, created male and female in his image, become "one flesh"[1]—both in the physical sense and in the deepest spiritual sense even if they're not themselves aware of it. The elements of complete faithfulness and commitment to the other person in marriage and the total abandonment to that person in sex are a picture of God's love for us. Sex is meant to be a physical expression of all of that.

So two people can experience the physical pleasure of the sexual act, but outside of the lifelong commitment of marriage, it lacks the vital and transcendent connection to God, which is really heartbreaking when you think about it. Human beings long for that connection with God, for ultimate meaning. Our souls are hungry for it, and it's as if we're feeding them cotton candy and sodas. It's like cracking open an eggshell and finding there's nothing inside. From the outside it looks like a real egg, full of the possibility of life. But when you examine it more closely, you see it's just a hollow shell.

Q: Isn't saying that sex is intended for married couples the primary argument Christians use to justify treating homosexuals like second-class citizens?

A: Some Christians might use that argument as a moral battering ram in the debate over homosexuality. But that's certainly not the spirit of Jesus. To Jesus, and to anyone who says they are followers of his, the very idea of anyone being a second-class citizen is repugnant. We are all utterly equal in God's eyes, and anyone who knows God knows that too. Jesus spoke the truth to everyone, but whatever he said, he said in love and out of compassion.

Q: They why do some Christians say that God hates gay people?

A: It's a huge stretch to think anyone saying that could possibly be a Christian. God does not hate. Even when our behavior is contrary to his will, as everyone's is at some point, God still loves us more than we can imagine. Any loving parent knows that real love is unconditional, and God is the ultimate loving Parent. But because of his love for us, he's also against anything that would harm us.

Q: But don't many of the people who speak hatefully on this subject call themselves Christians?

A: Of course. But all sorts of monsters have called themselves Christians. When Christians behave like true Christians, meaning that they pattern their lives on the life of Jesus, they don't condemn anyone. To love someone is to treat them with the full dignity that every human deserves. And that holds true especially when we disagree with the other person. Jesus commands his followers to love their enemies. That's not negotiable.

You and I both know that Christians often fail to love others as Jesus commands. In this instance, we need to avoid confusing God and his teachings with the failures of Christians—or so-called Christians or self-proclaimed Christians—and their mistaken reading of Scripture. People have done all sorts of things in the name of Christianity that had nothing to do with Christianity or with God's will. It's a terrible mistake to assume that God condones bigotry or hypocrisy on the part of his children. He simply doesn't, and anyone who has a real relationship with God and serves him with their whole life doesn't condone it either.

Q: So what is the real Christian view of homosexuals?

A: The Christian view of homosexuals is that in God's eyes they are no different from anyone else. Just like Mother Teresa and Saint Paul and Billy Graham and every other human being, they are sinners in need of God's grace and forgiveness.

Q: You're saying that saints are sinners?

A: Of course. Every human being is a sinner, and we all need to be saved by the grace of Jesus Christ.[2] People struggling with sexual sins are no different in this regard. It's highly likely that some of the men and women we call saints struggled with sexual issues just as people do today.

Q: But Christians seem to put homosexuality into a special category somehow. I've heard some argue that homosexual desires—even if you don't act on them—are sinful.

A: Some Christians might believe that, but they're mistaken. Being tempted is not a sin. We've all been tempted to do any number of things that we didn't act on. We've considered lying, cheating, stealing, doing things to hurt someone else—but then we resisted the temptation. And of course Jesus himself was tempted in various ways! The difference was that he *never* gave in to temptation.[3] We have to be clear: we aren't sinning until we give in to temptation. Merely being tempted to sin is not sin.

Q: So having sexual desires is all right as long as you don't pursue them in a sinful way?

A: Sexual desire itself is a gift from God, but it has to be redeemed and used according to God's will. There are forms of sexual desire that constitute temptations to sin. Those would include a desire to have sex with anyone other than one's spouse. Of course, those desires are common and are evidence of our brokenness, of humanity's fall from grace. The same is true of any desire to do anything that is sin—whether it's greed or gluttony or laziness. So a sexual desire for someone of the same sex is a disposition toward sin, just as a heterosexual desire for someone other than one's spouse is a disposition toward sin, and how many of us can say we've never had such desires?

Every single human being is predisposed to resist God's will in various ways. We are all broken, and everyone has some kind of struggle. The question is not *whether* we struggle but with *what* we struggle. We are all broken in slightly different ways. So we can't judge one kind of brokenness as being superior to another or as being more objectionable than another. We are all equally in need of God's grace and healing. That's been the teaching of the Christian faith from the beginning, but people will always twist it and get it wrong.

Q: But why?

A: I can think of two reasons. First, it's a temptation for just about all of us to point at other people's problems and struggles in a way that makes us feel superior to them. We tend to look around and think, *I'm not as bad as that other guy.* Humans have been doing that since we left Eden. But God always opposes that sort of behavior. Jesus thundered against the Pharisees for doing it in his day. God won't let people get away with pretending they're better than anyone else.

Q: You said there were two reasons...

A: The other one I had in mind was that many Christians don't really know what the Bible says, so they take their cues from the wider culture, which is certainly not Christian. The culture will always be up and down, changing its stance on any number of issues from premarital sex to divorce to homosexuality to adultery. But God's point of view doesn't change.

Fifty years ago the culture demonized people who struggled with homosexual desires, and many in the church joined in the condemnation, to their shame. Likewise many churches supported racial segregation, simply going along with the accepted social standards at that time in their part of the country. But that's not what Scripture teaches. Anyone who knows the love of God is obliged to reach out to people who are different, those who are shunned, and those who are struggling with their sexuality. And, as we said, sexual struggles come in many forms—not just homosexuality.

Q: I don't see how people who are married struggle with their sexuality.

A: There are many ways someone who is married could struggle with sexual sin. Most married men struggle with sexual desires for women other than their wives. And even if a man is predisposed to treat his wife like a sexual object, like someone he doesn't love in the way Jesus loves the church, that man is acting out of his brokenness, not out of God's love. A woman who is longing for intimacy with a person beside her own spouse is struggling too. But even if people aren't struggling in sexual areas, they are struggling in other ways. All humans struggle with sin. Again, it's not a matter of if someone struggles; it's only a matter of how and with what. There are no exceptions.

Q: Still, you're saying no one could legitimately act on homosexual desires.

A: Which is one reason why those who claim to follow Jesus should have a particular compassion for anyone who struggles in this area! Anyone who is not struggling with this can hardly imagine how difficult it must be, especially for people living in a culture that either condemns them outright—or that tells them to "celebrate their sexuality" indiscriminately. They are presented with a false choice between these two unbiblical ideas. It's tragic and horribly unfair to anyone honestly trying to deal with this issue.

But a large part of the wider problem is that our society is absurdly focused on sex of all types. We've put so much emphasis on sexual gratification that we have trouble believing that the fulfillment of our sexual desires isn't the answer to all our problems. In line with that, we can hardly fathom the possibility that not all our sexual desires have to be gratified.

One way that Christians could help those who are struggling with sexual issues is to address this larger issue. We have reached the point where we think of sexual gratification as some kind of right instead of as a gift from God. This creates expectations that can never be met in anyone's life. Just because we have a desire doesn't mean it should be given in to. Every desire does not have to be satisfied. That's God's truth. But we live in a culture that can't handle the truth. Not in that area.

Q: But you said God put sexual desire in us, no?

A: Ultimately, sexual desire comes from God, yes. But we are broken human beings, and the realm of sexual desire is one of the main places where that brokenness manifests itself. So just because someone has a sexual desire certainly does not mean it's a God-given desire. Adulterous desires are not gifts from God. Would you tell a married man who wants to sleep with his neighbor or his secretary that he should act on that desire?

Q: I don't think so.

A: Most people wouldn't. We would tell him to suppress those desires, to work on his marriage, to love his wife. We would point out that adulterous desires are destructive and hurtful—to one's spouse and children and to the whole community. And certainly to oneself. But in our culture we often get the message that if you aren't happy in your marriage, you should look elsewhere. That's a destructive message, but it's very strong in the culture right now, and it's misled and hurt an awful lot of people.

Q: So you think people spend too much time thinking about sex?

A: Let's face it, our culture has elevated sex to such a preeminent status that we've effectively made it impossible for people to take seriously the idea that they should suppress any sexual desires. In a more emotionally mature culture, the idea wouldn't be nearly as difficult, but in our current culture—which seems stuck at an adolescent level on this subject—it's just about impossible. But if we care about people, we have to grow up and have a healthier attitude and stop talking in sound bites on something so profoundly important.

Q: Okay.

A: And let's be honest here. Many sexual desires are not only not God-given; they are dangerous.

Q: How can they be dangerous?

A: Just think about two examples: people who connect sex with violence and force, and those who have strong sexual desires toward children. If someone wants to force women to have sex or wants to have sex with children, we don't tell them that these are legitimate desires and they have a right to pursue them.

Q: Agreed.

A: And neither do we say that God made them that way. We tell those people to do everything necessary to avoid acting on their impulses. And when we find people acting on such desires, we prosecute them and imprison them to protect society.

In these two instances we have no problem with the idea that sexual gratification isn't a right. But it follows that if it's not a right for everyone, it's not a right for anyone. It's a gift from God, to be used in the way he intended it or not to be used at all.

Q: But you've used the most extreme examples to make your point. Most homosexual couples are adults having consensual sex, not predators or rapists.

A: Yes, and likewise a man who cheats on his wife in almost every instance is having sex with a willing partner. But we don't tell him that God made him that way and that his desire for other women should be acted on. And most of us wouldn't tell teenage boys or girls that they should act on their sexual desires.

God wants us to be healthy and fulfilled in life, so he tries to protect us from habits and behaviors that will harm us. It only follows logically that not all sexual desires come from God and not all sexual desires should be acted on. But our culture is so hypersexualized that we encourage people to "express themselves sexually" by acting on every desire.

We've adopted the terrible Freudian idea that sexual desire is at the core of everything and that suppressing sexuality is repressive and harmful.

Q: And it's not?

A: Of course not. From God's point of view, sex is a fragile and beautiful thing not to be treated roughly or indiscriminately. It is meant to be shared by a man and a woman in the lifelong commitment of marriage. That's what the biblical tradition has always understood as nonnegotiable, as one of the things that helps us live the life that God wants us to live and to find fulfillment in the deepest sense.

Q: Even if what you're saying is true, it doesn't explain why so many Christians single out homosexuals for condemnation.

A: There is only one consistent Christian view, and that is that God loves everyone and commands his followers to love everyone. Christians are to treat others as they would want to be treated if the shoe were on the other foot, with grace and compassion and the truth spoken *in love.* But Christians aren't always obedient to God's command to love others—especially those who are different.

Q: It seems that Christians like to zero in on an easy target, in this instance homosexuals, while conveniently ignoring bigger problems, such as corporate greed and pollution.

A: I couldn't agree more. Christians often overlook the destructive nature of gluttony, gambling, racism, drug or alcohol addiction, and greed. The good news is that God doesn't define us by our desires. He tells us we don't have to live at their mercy. We can be free of greed or gluttony or bigotry or an addiction. But you rarely hear this said about sexual desires. When it comes to the topic of sex, we avoid the logic of it. We choose not to think about the pain that is caused by unchecked sexual expression.

As I write this, it has been less than a year since a leading evangelical minister was dismissed from his pastorate after he confessed to sexual immorality. His confession came after a former male prostitute went public with allegations involving the minister. When a story such as this appears in the news, it reminds us that no one is exempt from sexual temptation. The debate over sexuality may not be easy, but perhaps both sides have finally learned enough about each other to participate with humility and civility, knowing that wherever we come out on it, we are genuinely all in it together, no exceptions.

9

Is Divorce Still a Sin?

Polygamy in the Bible; Why Marriages End

The New Testament was written in first-century Greek, and where English translations of the Bible use the word *love,* New Testament Greek uses four different words, each denoting a different kind of love. There is *eros,* which is romantic or sexual love; *philia,* which refers to the love in friendships and other relationships that are not romantic or erotic in nature; *storge,* which refers to the love between parents and children; and finally there is *agape,* which mostly refers to God's love, a love that is self-sacrificial and does not take self-interest into account.

The idea that self-sacrifice and not self-interest is at the heart of God's love for us is not a great surprise if we understand who God is or if we're in the process of finding out. But to discover that self-sacrifice and not self-interest is what God intends to be at the heart of our love for each other is another thing entirely and a rather big surprise indeed.

Q: You've said that God's requirement for marriage—and sex—is that it be limited to one man and one woman who are joined for life, right?

A: Just to be clear on this, it's not what I say. It's what the Christian faith has taught for two thousand years. But yes.

Q: But how can you say that when in the Bible you see lots of people—even God's favorites, such as King Solomon and King David—having multiple wives?

A: You're right. Polygamy doesn't exactly seem kosher, does it?

Q: It seems about as kosher as a cheeseburger with bacon. So how do you explain it?

A: It's a good question, and the answer has to do with something called God's "permissive will," which refers to things God allows but doesn't exactly endorse. You could say God puts up with certain things, but not because he approves of them.

Q: But how is it that some of his top guys got away with it?

A: The Bible gives us a picture of a certain culture at a certain time, without saying God approved of everything in it or that he considered that culture to be ideal. Polygamy is one of these things. Slavery is another. The cultures we read about in the Bible practiced these things, but God didn't approve of those practices.

Q: But don't you think it's odd that a hero of the Bible, such as David, didn't realize that polygamy was wrong?

A: Not necessarily. We all have blind spots. One hundred fifty years ago many Christians in this country owned slaves without seeming to understand the moral horror of it. And today many Christians use certain figures of speech, make financial decisions and entertainment choices, and do other things that would shock previous generations of Christians. So being unaware of moral or ethical restrictions and tolerating or even practicing things that go against God's will are part of being human. We will always fall short, including and especially Christians. But that doesn't mean people of faith shouldn't try to do everything we can to please God.

Q: What do Christians do today that you think would be the biggest shock to their spiritual ancestors?

A: Well, getting divorced would have to be right up there. Christians divorcing is about as prevalent today as it was rare and not accepted among Christians a hundred years ago.

Q: Are you saying divorce is a sin or that it's no longer considered a sin?

A: There's no question that God hates divorce. He says so in Malachi 2:16. Jesus also spoke very clearly and strongly against it.[1] But today Christians in the United States get divorced at about the same rate as everyone else. As you know, Christians get exercised about a lot of moral and political issues, but you don't hear them complaining too much about divorce.

Q: But if God hates divorce and if Jesus made a point of opposing it, then why do Christians freely engage in the practice? And what did Jesus say about it?

A: Whatever he said, he said in Aramaic. Do you mind if I give you the English translation?

Q: Ha. No.

A: Thanks. The best example of what he said is found in the gospel of Matthew. The Pharisees ask Jesus if he thinks divorce is permissible. Those asking the question are the religious leaders of Jesus' time, and they know the Scriptures backward and forward. So Jesus replies with what seems a tinge of sarcasm: "Haven't you read that at the beginning the Creator 'made them male and female'?" Of course they had read those words hundreds of times and almost certainly knew them by memory. Then Jesus continues by quoting Genesis again: "For this reason a man will leave his father and mother and be united to his wife, and the two will become one flesh." And then Jesus says the words we hear at almost every wedding ceremony: "So they are no longer two, but one. Therefore what God has joined together, let man not separate."[2] Usually we hear the King James wording, which says, "What therefore God hath joined together, let not man put asunder."[3]

Q: So that's where that comes from...

A: Yes. Those are Jesus' words. But the story's not finished, because after Jesus said what he said, the Pharisees pointed out that Moses had allowed divorce. They were implying that it was okay. And Jesus replied, "Moses permitted you to divorce your wives because your hearts were hard. But it was not this way from the beginning."[4] The provision that Moses made in the Old Testament is an example of God's permissive will. God disapproves of divorce, but he allows it. And then Jesus says to the Pharisees: "I tell you that anyone who divorces his wife, except for marital unfaithfulness, and marries another woman commits adultery."[5]

Q: Whoa. You don't hear that too often.

A: Exactly. It's much easier to concentrate on Bible verses that don't rub us the wrong way. As you have pointed out before, Christians find it easy to complain about an issue such as same-sex marriage. But ask them about Jesus' thoughts on divorce, and they're more likely to shuffle off to Buffalo and leave you hanging. It's very challenging to face the fact that Jesus would only allow divorce if a spouse has been unfaithful. Who wants to hear it?

Q: But are you saying that God wants people to spend the rest of their lives in unhappy marriages?

A: Unhappiness is never part of God's plan, but that doesn't mean we can throw out Jesus' words on the subject of divorce. He doesn't seem to suggest that unhappiness, terrible as that can be, is legitimate grounds for divorce. But I don't think that means he would want us to accept an unhappy marriage as something that can't be changed. People can work at difficult marriages, and many who do find that the situation improves dramatically. And in the process they usually learn a lot about themselves and their spouses. And of course that *is* part of God's plan for us. He wants us to learn to be less selfish, for one thing. And marriage is one of the places where we're able to see how selfish we can sometimes be.

Q: But what about a marriage that is worse than simply "unhappy"? What about a marriage without love?

A: What do you mean by that, a marriage "without love"? I think you're probably using a faulty and unbiblical definition of love.

Q: Okay, according to you what is love?

A: Forget about me. My definition of love is as sappy as anybody's. But let's talk about what God says on the subject.

Q: All right. What is God's definition of love?

A: The first thing is that, contrary to what you hear every day, love is not a feeling.

Q: You mean it's more than a feeling, like in the Foreigner song?

A: Didn't Boston record "More Than a Feeling"?

Q: Whoa. You're absolutely right! It was the first song on that cool album with the spaceships on the cover.

A: Anyway, yes! It's more than a feeling. A lot more. In fact, it's something else entirely. It really has nothing to do with feelings.

Q: You've lost me. What is love if not a feeling? How can it have nothing to do with feelings?

A: Well, not to be a downer, but the idea that love is a feeling is one of the most destructive lies in our whole confused culture. Think about Jesus' statement that we are to love our enemies.[6] Obviously he's not telling us to be "in love" with our enemies or to have romantic feelings toward them.

Q: Okay...

A: Jesus doesn't tell us to *feel* love for our enemies; he tells us to *act* lovingly toward them. He means we are to do unto our enemies what we would have them do unto us, *even if we don't feel like it.* He can't tell us how to feel, but he can and does tell us how to *act.* It's a command, and it's about behavior. So in God's eyes, love is about behavior, and our behavior is a choice. I might not be able to have loving feelings toward a particular person. In many cases, my feelings might not be under my control. But the way I act toward others is definitely under my control.

Q: So according to God, we <u>choose</u> love?

A: Ba-da-*bing*. Here's an example. I might be angry at my wife, but that doesn't justify acting or speaking in anger. I've promised to love her at all times, even when I don't feel like it. So, yes, love is a choice and an action. It's not something that just comes over me or something that comes and goes. Romantic feelings can come and go, but the love that God is talking about is much more than emotions and hormones.

The truth that love is an action and not a feeling is one of the most countercultural ideas imaginable. And the ramifications from this are absolutely huge. They touch everything.

Q: Like what?

A: Well, like marriage and divorce. If I believe love is a feeling, then when the feeling of love declines in marriage or even goes away entirely, I will think it's impossible to recapture love for my spouse. But if I understand that the feeling and the reality of loving someone are totally separate, the equation changes. I'm no longer a victim of circumstances or emotions.

Q: How so?

A: Think about the marriage vows. You stand in front of a crowd of people—and God—and you promise that you will love your spouse till death do you part. That means that death, and not a lack of loving feelings, is the only thing that will separate you. That's how God sees it, but we've allowed a bad cultural definition of love to swamp God's definition of love.

Q: So the spouses in a marriage without romantic feelings can still have hope?

A: Without question. First of all, with God all things are possible, and it's God's will that we do everything we can to save a marriage. He really will help us if we let him, and one way to invite God's help is to obey him by behaving lovingly even if our feelings are not what we'd like them to be. Chances are very good that if someone is behaving lovingly toward his or her spouse, the romantic feelings will return. But if we let the presence or absence of romantic feelings guide our behavior, we're at their mercy, and the marriage is on a foundation of quicksand.

Q: I have to admit, this is challenging stuff...

A: It's revolutionary when you realize we live in a culture that worships feelings and that has bought into this bad definition of love—hook, line, and sinker. Every movie and television program operates from this definition. But we have to stand against it, because it's so hurtful to so many people.

Q: Like what?

A: For one thing, with people believing that love is a feeling and not an action, the whole idea of marriage itself has been badly undermined. Christians who are upset about unmarried people sleeping together or about same-sex marriage have to understand that these things are a perfectly logical outgrowth of the idea that love is a feeling. It has done great damage to marriage and to our culture in general. It has confused millions of people who are trying to do their best with the bad definition they have been given—and that they see and hear everywhere.

But in large part Christians themselves are to blame for the situation. They bought the lie just as readily as everyone else did. Instead of getting up in arms over these other hot-button issues, people of faith might instead figure out how they got bamboozled into accepting a completely unbiblical idea of what love is. Because it's the root system of the whole sad tree. It's as if they've climbed up into the tree to cut off certain branches and have been hacking away with all their might, but the tree has been growing faster than Jack's beanstalk, and—alas!—they hardly want to look down and see how far from home they've come.

God created eros, or romantic love, but he never intended it to sustain lifelong relationships—and families. That is not its purpose. God created something infinitely more powerful to undergird and protect the lifelong commitment of marriage. It's the type of love the New Testament calls agape. Romantic love has hormones and biochemistry behind it, which can be powerful for a time, but it has very serious limits. In contrast, agape love has God behind it. To love self-sacrificially is to love others with God's love. When we do that, we are loving others with the same love that created the universe and sustains it today. If agape love can sustain the universe, it can probably sustain marriages too.

10

What Is Fundamentalism?

Faith and a Cannoli; Jesus on Water; the Nicene Creed

Frank Capra's *Mr. Smith Goes to Washington* has to be one of the most uplifting and patriotic films ever made. Jimmy Stewart plays Mr. Smith, the quintessential small-town hero who takes on the political machine of his home state, and during his famous filibuster on the Senate floor, he reads from, among other things, the Bible.

Popular culture portrays faith much differently today than it did in 1939. Today, people who take their faith seriously tend to be portrayed as either hypocritical or deranged—or even as evil or violent. In *The Da Vinci Code,* which was both a popular movie and one of the best-selling books of all time, the character who was the most serious about his faith was a self-flagellating and murderous monk. If the fact that he bloodied himself and killed people wasn't enough to make the point that he wasn't someone you'd see in a Norman Rockwell painting, the book's author made him an albino and named him Silas. You don't meet a lot of folks named Silas nowadays. And based on this movie, you probably wouldn't want to.

Q: We're always hearing about different types of fundamentalists in the news. How would you define a fundamentalist?

A: It's a word with a long history, so can I tell you a bit of its history?

Q: Of course.

A: And I'll need to use some food metaphors.

Q: Not a problem.

A: Okay, well, like many words that eventually fell on hard times, the words *fundamentalist* and *fundamentalism* started out in life showing great promise. They were rather positive terms when they were coined in the early twentieth century by Christians who wanted to reemphasize the "fundamentals" of the Christian faith. Of course, the people who wanted to reemphasize the fundamentals called themselves "fundamentalists."

Q: What made these people want to reemphasize the fundamentals?

A: In the second half of the nineteenth century, new developments in science—as well as new ways of understanding how to read the Bible—started challenging some of the basics of what the Bible taught. Darwinism, Marxism, and what was called higher criticism had a lot to do with it. Some of the central tenets of the Christian faith—the "fundamentals"—were being threatened.

Q: What specifically was being threatened?

A: Almost everything; all the big stuff. The belief that God created us. The belief that Jesus rose from the dead in his physical body. The belief that Jesus was actually God in human flesh and that Mary was a virgin when she gave birth to Jesus. The belief that the Bible was inspired by God and was therefore completely trustworthy. The belief that all the miracles in the Bible really happened. Pretty much the whole cannoli, so to speak. Many Christians didn't know how to respond to these challenges. The evidence from the realms of scientific inquiry and scholarly examination of the biblical texts seemed to contradict what the Bible was saying.

Q: So what happened?

A: There were two basic responses. One group, those who called themselves fundamentalists, rededicated themselves to the fundamentals of the faith. They set out to establish that these fundamentals are what Christianity is all about.

Q: What did the other group do?

A: They got rid of the fundamentals.

Q: Which ones?

A: All of them, really. They figured that progress was progress, and if much of what the Bible said wasn't really true, based on science and other types of research, they'd just have to accept that it wasn't true. They figured that maybe Christianity didn't really depend on things like the virgin birth and the incarnation and the resurrection and all the miracles and so on.

But this presented a huge problem. When you remove those things, you don't have much left. It's a lot like having a cannoli without the filling, which isn't just a problem; it's a tragedy! And if you don't know what cannoli are, that's a tragedy too, because they're unbelievable! But if I'm forced to describe the situation in noncannoli terms, I might say that it's like having a burrito with nothing inside but warm air.

Q: Qué lástima!

A: Exactly. But what's strange is that the people who were willing to discard the core Christian teachings still continued to call what was left "Christianity." A cannoli without the filling certainly wouldn't be called a cannoli, at least not in any bakery I would bother with. People can do what they want, and if they want a cannoli without the filling, that's their business. But they should call it something else. If I ordered a cannoli to go and got home and made a pot of coffee and when the coffee was ready, I opened the bag and saw that the cannoli had no filling, I would get pretty hot under the collar. I think it's safe to say I'd have a few words with the guy who sold it to me.

Q: What was he thinking?

A: Exactly.

Q: So you're saying that even without these "fundamentals," they continued to call it Christianity?

A: Yes, this one group of people did. They decided to redefine Christianity, to eliminate the miraculous stuff and instead to emphasize things such as helping people, feeding the poor, and so on. Of course atheists and agnostics and Hindus and Buddhists and everyone else can do those things too—and *should* do those things. They are all good things. But there was no real reason to call doing them "Christianity." The good deeds had become divorced from the Bible. Jesus had become a mere role model. It was as if people no longer needed to worship him as God but still felt they had to do the things he said to do.

Q: Are you saying Jesus without miracles is not really Jesus?

A: If you take away his divinity and his ability to miraculously heal the sick and raise the dead and command the wind and the waves to stop, then you're also taking away his ability to pay for our sins on the cross and to rise from the dead. You're essentially left with a really nice guy who teaches morals and ethics and hands out bread and fish to large numbers of people. But he doesn't do it miraculously. If you take away the supernatural stuff, there's not much left that's very compelling.

Q: It sounds like a very different Jesus...

A: It is. And without these fundamentals, the Bible ends up being something very different too. It came to be seen as a book filled with prescriptions for social action and a collection of exaggerated folk stories and anecdotes that never really happened. But you get to wondering: if the biblical accounts are full of exaggerations and untruths, why bother with any of it? You really couldn't know which parts were just old-fashioned nonsense and which parts were worth taking seriously. In some ways you'd be better off reading *Grimm's Fairy Tales* or the Greek myths, because at least they didn't claim to be true.

The people who were willing to discard the supernatural elements of the Bible had invented what came to be known as the "social gospel." Many people were interested in helping others and improving society, and they felt that was the real point of Christian faith, so the supernatural stuff didn't really matter. Much of mainstream Christianity became influenced by the social gospel. Standing up to new scientific discoveries was just too difficult, or so it seemed, so they figured they'd adopt the "if you can't beat 'em, join 'em" philosophy.

Q: And the fundamentalists, as you said, were the folks who took the opposite view.

A: Right. They saw that this other group was watering down Christian faith by radically redefining it away from its historical roots and core beliefs. So the fundamentalists reasserted the fundamentals. You might say they wanted to reemphasize the nonnegotiable importance of the filling to the cannoli.

Q: And you might not...

A: I'm sorry, but I could so go for a cannoli right about now... but I'll try to forget about it till the end of the chapter.

Q: Thank you.

A: Anyway, the fundamentalists weren't saying anything new. It was the same thing Christians had believed since the beginning of the faith. It was all in the Nicene Creed, for example. But eventually they came up with a list of five basic fundamentals.

Q: And they were?

A: Number one: that the Holy Spirit inspired and guided the writers of the Bible and that the Bible is without error. Number two: that Mary was a virgin when she gave birth to Jesus. Number three: that Jesus' death on the cross was a sacrifice for us—he died in our place, and we are reconciled to God because of his sacrifice. (This includes the idea that we are separated from God spiritually by our sins and that only through what Jesus did on the cross can we be restored to a right relationship with God.)

Q: Keep going.

A: Number four: that Jesus rose from the dead—and that his body, not just his spirit, rose from the grave.

Q: Okay, what else?

A: Number five: that God's miracles are real miracles.

Q: What do you mean "real" miracles? What's a fake miracle?

A: A fake miracle is a miracle that the Bible presents as a miracle but that science would try to explain away as a natural phenomenon. Do you remember the passage in the Gospels where Jesus walked on water?

Q: Of course. It's kind of famous.

A: Okay, well, that would be called a real miracle, walking on water. But just last year an article in several major newspapers claimed that the water Jesus walked on was frozen.

Q: As in ice?

A: Exactly, the kind Zambonis smooth out. The news articles claimed Jesus had walked on ice! And they weren't joking. That's an example of a fake miracle. Because if that's all Jesus did, then he didn't do anything. It might be difficult to believe that Jesus walked on water, but it's not nearly as difficult as understanding why anyone would care about a man who did nothing more than walk on ice.[1]

Q: Yeah, why would he be a revered religious leader?

A: If Jesus walked on *ice,* I think we're pretty safe in ignoring him. Can you imagine? Somehow it seems to me that someone who is the Messiah and God incarnate is probably not the sort of person who is going to slip and slide across the ice and try to pass it off as a miracle! But that's what folks who are promoting such ideas seem to be saying. The idea is far more implausible than the idea of the Creator of the universe being able to walk on water.

Q: Got it.

Q: If the fundamentalists just wanted to emphasize the historic teachings of Christianity, how did they get such a bad reputation?

A: It's complicated, but at some point anything that was seen as anti-intellectual and Bible-thumping was labeled "fundamentalist." It became a catchall term of derision. The fact is that anyone who believes in historic, orthodox Christianity is a fundamentalist. But then the word took on an even more negative connotation in 1979 when terrorists took Americans hostage at the embassy in Teheran. The news media described the hostage takers as Muslim fundamentalists, which planted the idea that a religious fanatic of any kind is a fundamentalist. So the original idea behind the word, which was simply a group of folks who wanted to reassert the basics of the Christian faith, was completely lost.

Q: Interesting.

A: Today most Christians who believe in historic, orthodox Christianity have shied away from the term. They've adopted other terms, such as *evangelical* or *born again* or *theologically orthodox.* If you believe the five fundamentals, which are the basics of the faith, then you are a Christian. You don't need an adjective. And if you don't believe the five fundamentals, it's fair to say that you can't rightfully consider yourself a Christian according to the historical definition of the word. You might be a very nice person—perhaps much nicer than some of the folks who do believe those things—but you can't honestly use the term *Christian.*

It doesn't matter whether you go to a Catholic, Orthodox, or Protestant church, those are the fundamentals of the Christian faith—what C. S. Lewis called "mere Christianity." But you don't have to refer specifically to this list of five fundamental beliefs. If you're more comfortable with saying that you believe the Nicene Creed, you could do that.

Q: Now that you mention it, what exactly is the Nicene Creed?

A: Actually, the fundamentals of the faith and the Nicene Creed are closely related. It's ironic that in the early twentieth century, a bunch of American Protestants had to reassert the same basics that had been clarified in the fourth century in Nicaea. The Nicene Creed is the formal statement of faith that was put together in AD 325 at a church council convened by the emperor Constantine. A creed is a statement of belief. The word comes from the Latin word *credo* meaning "belief."

Q: But why is the Nicene Creed so important?

A: Just to be clear, the Nicene Creed is the one that goes: "We believe in one God, Father Almighty, Maker of heaven and earth and of all things seen and unseen, and in one Lord, Jesus Christ, the only begotten Son of God, begotten not created, Light of Light, True God of True God, of one essence with the Father, through Whom all things were made..." and so on.[2]

Q: Got it. But why is it so important? Why do so many churches recite it week after week?

A: It's a superconcise statement of Christian belief. It certainly doesn't sum up everything Christians believe, but it's the essence—or a distillation, you could say—of what constitutes Christian belief.

Q: Why did it take until AD 325 for such a statement to be put together? Hadn't Christianity existed for three centuries at that point? What did they believe before then?

A: Christians had always believed what the Nicene Creed says, from the beginning. The real point of having the church council and of writing the creed was to put in writing what Christian belief had always been. That way, people wouldn't have to debate it every few years.

Q: Are you sure it wasn't just a way for the people at the council to get their version of Christianity adopted as the official party line?

A: You probably heard that in *The Da Vinci Code,* right?

Q: How did you know that? That's spooky.

A: Just a wild guess. But it's not even one percent true. It's crazy talk. You do keep hearing it, though, and I think it has something to do with the fact that some people don't like what Christianity represents—or what they think it represents—so they grab at anything they think will undermine it. *The Da Vinci Code* played into a lot of those feelings. Everything in that book has been soundly debunked, but some people have been hurt either by the church or by Christians, and they have very strong feelings in this regard.

Q: Okay, what exactly happened at the Council of Nicaea?

A: As I said, the point of the council was to set down once and for all what everyone had already believed for three centuries. The council clarified Christian belief and weeded out false beliefs so that nothing would deviate from the core beliefs that Christians had held from day one.

Q: Why wouldn't they consider new input?

A: That's a legitimate question, but ultimately the creed is not about new ideas or old ideas. It's about truth itself, and truth is outside of time. There's really no "new" truth. All truth is eternal. It has always existed. "One plus one equals two" has always been true. It will never "evolve" to something else or fall out of fashion. You might get tired of it, but if you change it, the entire universe might crack and fall to pieces. You can't monkey with absolute truth. One plus one can't suddenly equal two point one. It would affect everything. Bridges would fall down.

Q: Pants too.

A: Right. Anyway, when you're talking about the nature of God and things that have to do with his nature, you're not talking about things that can change even if you want them to. They are immutable and eternal.

Q: What does that have to do with the creed?

A: It gets back to the truth of what Christianity is and who Jesus is. Either Jesus is God, or he's not. Either the teachings and beliefs of the Bible were always true and always will be true, or they were never true. Either Jesus rose from the dead bodily, or he didn't. Either he was born of a real virgin, or he wasn't. If these things were true when Jesus was alive, three hundred years before the council, then they were still true in AD 325.

The Council of Nicaea was not about a power-hungry group of churchmen convening to get their pet ideas set into stone. They wanted to clear up any misunderstandings that people might have on the key theological issues. That had never been done before by a group that consisted of virtually all the Christian leaders in the world. It's really pretty amazing when you think of it.

Q: Well, that clears up a few things.

A: And now, I believe I have an important appointment with a cannoli. *Ciao.*

In *The Da Vinci Code,* one of the most popular books in recent times, the Christian faith is portrayed as a vast conspiracy of lies, all thought up by devious, power-hungry hypocrites and murderers. Is it any wonder that the idea of being serious about the Christian faith isn't something most people would want anything to do with?

11

If Jesus Was God, Wasn't He Immune from Pain?

God in Human Form; the Torture of Crucifixion; Jesus Choosing to Suffer

Mel Gibson's *The Passion of the Christ* was one of the most controversial movies ever to hit American theaters, and when it made $600 million, most critics found themselves wondering what exactly they had missed. Why would people pay money to see misery heaped upon misery? What was the point? Some audiences pay money to see slasher films and get cheap thrills from the horror and gore, but this was something else entirely. This was, after all, a religious film.

The answer may lie in the fact that, for many, the movie wasn't a movie at all, at least not in the conventional sense. It wasn't really meant as entertainment or even as something educational in the same way that some other disturbing films can be. *The Passion of the Christ,* it seems, was meant—and was taken by many—to be a kind of religious devotional. Scores of past generations had stared for hours at icons of the bloodied, suffering Christ, meditating on his agonies that they might understand his painful sacrifice for them. Such icons were principally meant as aids to devotion. They are thought of as works of art only by those who miss their creators' original intention.

It seems that for many in our generation, Gibson's controversial movie was a contemporary version of what icons were for previous generations. It was a two-hour devotional, neither entertaining nor educational, but upsetting, sobering, and finally cathartic, the way a wake or a funeral can be. We certainly don't enjoy such things, but of course they aren't meant to be enjoyed.

Q: Many Christians make a big deal about how terrible the crucifixion was. I don't mean to sound sacrilegious, but if Jesus is God, wasn't his dying on the cross actually not such a big deal for him?

A: I'm not following.

Q: Since he had divine power, and also because he knew that anytime he wanted he could save himself, don't you think crucifixion was different for him than it was for ordinary mortals?

A: Oh, I get it. This is a great question. And it's very important. Okay, here's the deal: when Jesus left heaven, he voluntarily gave up the glory that belonged to him in order to take on human flesh and dwell on earth.[1] In other words, *he really and truly became a human being.* Jesus wasn't God pretending to be a man; he was God who had actually become a man.

Q: Okay...

A: So he wasn't in any way immune to ordinary human limitations, like getting tired or feeling disappointed or being tempted to sin or experiencing physical pain. He wasn't a mythical superhero. Which means that when he was brutally whipped and bloodied before the crucifixion, it was just as painful for him as it would be for you or me. And when they drove the spikes through his hands and feet and raised him up on the cross, he suffered just as much as anyone would.

Q: But if he was God, couldn't he have decided to rescue himself anytime he wanted?

A: Your question implies that somehow because he was God, there was an easy out for him if things got too intense. But there wasn't, and that's important to understand. The torture of crucifixion hurt Jesus just as much as it would hurt any of us. But he was given a choice, and he chose to go through with it. There was no easy out.[2] But he deliberately chose it anyway, because he knew that it was the only way to bring you and me into heaven with him. And to say he could have come down from the cross is no different than saying to a father who is being tortured instead of his own children that he could just get up anytime and be done with the suffering. Of course, technically he could do that. But could he *really*, considering what's at stake?

Q: What do you mean?

A: I mean, if the choice would be that his child would be tortured and killed instead of him, could he really just say,

"Okay, I've had enough. Go ahead and torture the kid. I'm out of here"? No loving parent could ever do that. They would rather suffer the tortures of the damned than let their kids go through it. And that's exactly what Jesus did. To come off the cross would have been to put you and me *on* the cross. That was the deal.[3] He understood that.

Q: I admit I've never thought of it that way.

A: Most folks haven't, but it changes things when you give this some careful thought. Jesus did have a choice, and it was an extraordinarily unpleasant one: he could either save you and me or save himself. Someone had to suffer and die to pay for our sins. And because of how much he loved you, he didn't really have a choice. He loved you and still loves you far more than he loved comfort or safety or avoiding pain himself. He chose to save you and not to save himself.

And keep in mind there was no crowd cheering him on and telling him what a great thing he was doing for humanity. Instead, people were mocking him. In fact some were saying, "He saved others; let him save himself if he is the Christ of God, the Chosen One."[4]

Q: Honestly, I've thought the same thing. If he was in fact the Son of God, he <u>could</u> have done that.

A: The important thing is that he chose not to. He chose to save us—even the people who were jeering and mocking him—instead of saving himself.

It's important to realize how much it cost Jesus to be crucified. It was not some easy, symbolic act. If one of your parents or your spouse or a dear friend had done the same thing for you, you wouldn't shrug it off as a mythic event, as something historic and distant. To watch someone you love suffer that way, in your place, would break your heart, would haunt you forever. We need to try to see the crucifixion in the same light; otherwise, we take it for granted.

What Jesus did for us is not just an interesting idea. We tend to think about the crucifixion in theoretical terms, as if Jesus lets us keep him at arm's length. We prefer not to think of the human reality of his suffering. We're okay with it as a story but not as a horrible reality. Jesus wasn't an idealized superhuman. He was every bit as real as we are—and that was the whole point of his coming to earth. That's what *incarnation* means—God taking on human flesh.

Q: Are you saying that Jesus' suffering is proof that God really did become a human or that Jesus really is God?

A: Both. But there's more. If Jesus hadn't been as fragile as we are, his suffering would have cost him much less pain, and our gratitude to him would be negligible. But if we see him as he actually was and understand that he did this for us just the same as if our own parent or spouse had done this for us, it is devastating and unspeakably heartbreaking, and it floods us with gratitude and a desire to do anything we can to love him back. What he has done puts us forever in his debt, and the more we see what he has done, the more we want to spend our lives living for him, loving him with our whole being.

Q: That's a different story.

A: When you see it for what it really is, suddenly you see why Jesus' crucifixion and resurrection have been called the greatest story ever told. If you understand the reality of this, you can't help but see that it's the one story in the world that has the power to change each of our stories forever.

Q: You've talked about how horrible the crucifixion was, but doesn't the Bible say that everything—even the worst stuff—works out for the best?

A: No.

Q: No? I thought it was in the Bible... Are you sure it's not?

A: I'm sure. Of course, you hear this said over and over, and people agree to it without realizing what it really means. The basic idea behind this saying is that we shouldn't worry because somehow everything will turn out fine. I'm sorry to say it, but that idea—in the parlance of G-rated films—is pure, unadulterated horsefeathers.

Q: So you're saying it's not true.

A: How'd you guess?

Q: But it seems like such a nice idea! What's the problem with it?

A: The problem is that it seems like such a nice idea. It's much *too* nice, in fact, because it doesn't deal with the problem of evil, which is *not* so nice. Evil is real, and because of it, things are profoundly messed up. The amount of suffering and misery around us can't be dealt with by a cheesy platitude such as "all things work out for the best in the end." If your kids were kidnapped and sold into slavery and you knew you'd never see them again, you would see the lie in "all things work out for the best in the end." If you were living in Germany during World War II and your loved ones were loaded onto a boxcar with other people from your neighborhood to be shipped off to Treblinka or Buchenwald or Auschwitz, how would you feel if someone told you all things work out for the best? What if someone you loved was about to be lynched for the color of his skin? To say such a thing to someone in the midst of great suffering wouldn't just be insensitive and rude—it would be wrong.

Q: But doesn't the Bible say something like that—that everything works out for the best?

A: It says *something* like that but not *that.*

Q: Then what does it say, exactly?

A: First, let me give you the background to what it says. The Bible doesn't equivocate on the existence of evil and on the fundamental brokenness at the heart of creation. Things in this world are not the way God wanted them to be. There is frightening injustice and unspeakable suffering and misery. And even the best of us, with the best intentions, end up doing things that hurt other people and ourselves. At the core of the Bible is the idea that this is an incalculably huge problem, the magnitude of which cannot be overstated. On the other hand...

Q: I'm glad there's more...

A: Me too. On the other hand, God has a plan to redeem the brokenness of the world—even the painful, senseless stuff. Everything that has been ruined can be redeemed. This is the good news of Jesus Christ, the central message of the Scriptures. But it doesn't sort of just happen!

Q: What do you mean "it doesn't sort of just happen"? Why doesn't it?

A: Because in order for it to happen, God has to first send his Son to die a gruesome and protracted torture-death. We can't forget that. Nothing can ever really "work out for the best" without that happening first.

Q: But that has already taken place, no? Jesus died two thousand years ago.

A: Yes, it happened. But we have to remember the unspeakably terrible price Jesus paid to make it happen—the suffering and the death. We can't take that for granted, as though it happened two thousand years ago and now we don't need to think about it. The price that was paid so you and I and the world could somehow be redeemed is beyond our wildest reckoning. It's simply unfathomable. We can never think of it enough. And we have to accept that sacrifice, have to let it sink deeply into our souls.

Q: Fair enough. But you said there is something in the Bible about things working out for the best. I didn't dream that, did I?

A: No. The verse is Romans 8:28, but if you don't read the entire verse, the meaning is distorted. It says that "in all things God works for the good of those who love him, who have been called according to his purpose." Another translation says, "all things work together for good, for those who are called according to his purpose."[5] In other words, *if* we enter into the will of God and *if* we accept his love for us and allow ourselves to be used by him, then all the things that happen to us, even the worst things, can be woven into a tapestry that is ultimately beautiful and glorious. Usually, this happens in a way we can't really comprehend. But that's a far cry from the bumper-sticker shallowness that says "everything will work out in the end."

And keep in mind the precondition of God's working things for our ultimate good. We first have to enter into the will of God, which involves setting aside our own agendas and our selfish desires. We have to "lay down our lives," as Jesus did. If we're going to participate in God's work of redemption, we have to submit ourselves to his will. Defeating evil doesn't just happen, and our problems don't just "work out." Only if we seriously choose to follow God's will is it possible for things to work out to our ultimate good.

If we have entrusted our lives to God and are constantly

turning our difficulties over to him, then we really can know that all things will work out in the end. If we are living that way and trusting Jesus, then the Bible says we are not to worry.[6] For those who have accepted Jesus and understand the magnitude of his sacrifice for us, all things really do work out for the good. But if we really understand it, we will entrust our whole lives to God and to his purposes. We will enter into Jesus' obedience toward his heavenly Father. We will die to self, just as Jesus did, and will live for God. We can end up at that place, but it's via a very different route than most people expect. It's the route that goes straight through the cross and leads to life and hope.

Jesus' death on the cross is the supreme metaphor. One might rightly conclude that all meaning in the universe radiates outward from this one event. Without it, everything else is hopelessly fractured and absurd. But with it, all is united in the love of God.

To what can such a thing be compared? A century and a half ago a single golden railroad spike connected the American East and West and changed the world. But compared to the cross, even that grand image is hopelessly inadequate. Twenty centuries ago three spikes of iron crucified God incarnate, and in so doing connected all things that were ever apart and needed connecting. In the cross, every chasm is bridged and every wound is healed. The past is reconciled to the future and the beginning to the end, and we are again reconciled to ourselves and to each other and to God forever.

12

Isn't the Resurrection Meant to Be Symbolic?

Fact vs. Symbol; the Idea of Jesus Rising in Your Heart

Late one night in 1930, in some woods behind Magdalen College in Oxford, England, C. S. Lewis and his friend J. R. R. Tolkien were walking and talking with another friend, Hugo Dyson. Lewis was the only one in the group who wasn't a Christian. He had abandoned his atheism but was still far from accepting the strange idea that the Creator of the vast universe had been born in a certain part of the Roman Empire two thousand years earlier. Lewis and Tolkien shared a deep love of Norse mythology, and as they walked and talked long past midnight, Tolkien explained to Lewis that the story of Jesus was just like one of those hauntingly beautiful myths. He dared Lewis to imagine that once in history a myth had actually been true.

Could the story of Jesus be that one true myth?

Q: Is it okay to believe that the resurrection of Jesus was a symbol?

A: It *is* a symbol.

Q: Then it's all right if we don't believe he literally rose from the dead?

A: Oh, I see... You're asking if it's okay to believe that it was *only* symbolic. The answer to that question is no; the resurrection wasn't *only* symbolic. It took place historically and physically. A corpse returned to life, miraculously. That's a rather important detail. If you don't believe that part of the story, then you can't have anything resembling actual Christianity.

Q: But why? Isn't the symbolic idea of the resurrection what's really important instead of whether it did or didn't happen, which we can never really know anyway?

A: There is no question that the symbolic idea behind the resurrection is intriguing. But whether the resurrection really happened is what matters beyond all else. If it didn't really happen, then the symbolic aspect of it falls apart too. If it wasn't a real event, in which a dead body miraculously rose from the grave and came to life, then it's not really worth talking about much—except as an embarrassment. The entire Christian faith depends on its having actually happened—literally—so, no, it's not what we'd call optional.

Q: But why? I don't have any problem with it not being a literal miracle.

A: You *would* if you understood the implications. First, the Bible says Jesus rose from the dead physically. It makes this claim repeatedly and very clearly.[1] So if it actually *didn't* happen, then the Bible itself is telling lies and cannot be inspired by God. If that's the case, we can all pack up our peanut-butter-and-jelly sandwiches and head for the hills. Either Jesus really did rise from the dead, or the Bible is fatally undermined. Jesus' physical resurrection is at the center of it all.

Q: It sounds as though you're putting way too much emphasis on just one event in the Bible. Why should everything else hang on this one isolated incident?

A: Because it's far from an isolated incident; it's the hinge incident. Saint Paul explains in the book of 1 Corinthians that if the resurrection *didn't* happen, then everything is lost: "If Christ has not been raised, our preaching is useless and so is your faith.... And if Christ has not been raised, your faith is futile; you are still in your sins."[2] Without the resurrection, there is no meaning in Christianity. Without the resurrection, you're wasting your time to have faith in Jesus.

If Paul knew the resurrection was nothing more than a powerful story with rich symbolic meaning, he could have saved face by not insisting on its literal truth. He could have couched his terms differently to give himself a convenient way out, an escape hatch in case it was later proved beyond question that Jesus had not risen from the dead. He could have hedged his bet and at least given himself some wiggle room. But he did just the opposite. He knew that it had happened, and he met and talked with many of the people who actually had seen Jesus after he had been crucified and who had spoken with him and who had touched him.[3] So Paul is as emphatic as can be that it actually happened. He believed this one thing so strongly that he insists that if it isn't true, everything he's talking about is a sham.

Q: Okay, but humor me. Just for the sake of argument, why couldn't Jesus have risen figuratively—in the hearts of his disciples, as I've heard said?

A: The idea of Jesus "rising in the hearts of his disciples," when you really break it down, is a kind of nonstatement. It *seems* like a statement, but it's really nothing more than a dodge. It sounds very *spiritual,* as if there should be deep and dramatic meaning there. But at the end of the day, it's an empty phrase masquerading as the answer to one of the most important questions ever asked.

Q: What do you mean it doesn't mean anything?

A: It's like saying "Your check is in the mail—metaphorically!" Or "Let me carry that heavy box for you—*in my mind.*" It's meaningless. What would it mean for someone to "rise in the hearts" of others? We need to ask that question, because otherwise we're just accepting a spiritual-sounding cliché that doesn't mean anything. We can't be afraid to demand real answers, even if we fear that everyone else will think we're stupid or unspiritual. But we're not stupid or unspiritual at all; we're only insisting on real answers to important questions. The question about Jesus' rising from the dead is one question that has a superclear answer when you read what the Bible says. There's no mistaking it.

Q: And the superclear answer you refer to is the literal interpretation of this event?

A: Yes, accepting the account in the Gospels at face value. In this case, it's an answer that makes some people uncomfortable, so they try to cover up the whole thing by substituting a phony, pseudospiritual kind of answer, such as saying "Jesus rose in the hearts of his disciples." That is an answer that should satisfy no one. It's similar to when an older movie actress is filmed through gauze to hide her wrinkles. A pseudospiritual answer attempts to smooth out the claims of the Bible that are hard to accept. But we need to look at the question, wrinkles and all, to remove any layers of confusion. Either Jesus rose from the dead physically, or he didn't. If he did rise bodily from the grave, it means that everything Jesus said and taught is true and powerful and life changing and world changing.

Q: That does raise the stakes a bit.

A: This whole resurrection question is like standing in the middle of railroad tracks and playing chicken with a locomotive. Either the train stops, or you die. Everybody gets that, and there is no more discussion. It's the same with the question we're talking about: either Jesus rose from the dead bodily—and conquered death forever, including physical death and spiritual death—or he didn't. And if he didn't, then when we die, we just die. No resurrection, no heaven, no living forever in God's presence. It's simple, and a bit scary. But as I say, many folks want to hedge their bets. It's as if they're willing to play chicken with a locomotive but only if it's a "spiritual" locomotive, not a real one. After all, they don't want to be flattened.

We'd all like to hedge our bets, but Christianity won't let us. If you need convincing, read *Basic Christianity* by John Stott.[4] Some folks don't believe Jesus could have risen from the dead because they don't believe he really was God, but they like enough about the Christian story that they want to cling to the basic Christian narrative in some vague, nonthreatening form. But that's a little like standing in front of the locomotive as it bears down on you and refusing to accept that it's a real locomotive. There are some things you don't want to play chicken with.

J. R. R. Tolkien's late-night suggestion that the story of Jesus could be a true myth was compelling to C. S. Lewis, but he wasn't quite persuaded by it. A few days later, as Lewis rode to the Whipsnade Zoo in the sidecar of his brother's motorcycle, the thought came back to him. Lewis said that when he got into the sidecar, he didn't believe Jesus was the Son of God, but somehow—though he wasn't sure quite how—by the time they arrived at the zoo and he got out, he did.

13

What Are Things Like in Heaven?

Eternity, Not Time; a Person's Age in Heaven; Why Heaven Isn't Boring; Turtle Funerals

Years after his conversion to the Christian faith, C. S. Lewis wrote a brilliant allegorical novel about a bus ride from hell to heaven. It's called *The Great Divorce.* Heaven is portrayed as somehow more real and solid than our own world, and our world is portrayed as more real and solid than hell. In comparison to heaven's world of bright colors and light and solidity, our world is like a world of shadows and ghosts. God is ultimate reality, so the closer one gets to God, the more vivid and light-filled and solid things are. The farther away one goes from God, the less anything can really be said to exist at all.

In one scene, Lewis describes some of the visitors from hell getting out of the bus in heaven. They have difficulty walking on the grass because it's so solid and they are so inconsequential that their footsteps aren't heavy enough to push it down. In another scene, Lewis describes the visitors from hell as "man-shaped stains on the brightness of that air."[1] For anyone who wants to think in a new way about what heaven might be like, *The Great Divorce* is one of the best places to begin.

Q: I assume you believe that heaven actually exists.

A: I do. It does.

Q: All right, then I was hoping you might provide some specifics.

A: Oh sure. Not a problem. It's stpete777@heaven.org. If that bounces back, you might try PrlyG8s@heaven.org. I don't think he minds that I give it out.

Q: Ha. I wasn't asking for Saint Peter's e-mail address!

A: Are you sure?

Q: Yes! I just wanted to know how old people will be in heaven.

A: Oh. That's easy. Thirty-seven and a half.

Q: No kidding?

A: Actually, I am kidding. It's just that so many of these questions have complicated answers. I wanted one to be simple, like "What's the capital of North Dakota?"

Q: Bismarck?

A: Right. And wasn't that a nice feeling to come up with the answer just like that?

Q: Yes. But I still don't know how old people will be in heaven.

A: The answer, as I say, is a bit complicated, because any specific number of years, like thirty-seven, is an earthbound, time-bound concept.

Q: What do you mean by that?

A: Our world—and in fact, the entire universe—is inside time. But God and heaven are outside of time, existing in eternity. You might recall that we talked about this earlier.

Q: Of course. So God resides in a place that lasts forever?

A: Actually, *forever* doesn't even begin to cover it. Most people think eternity means a very, very long time. But billions and billions of years is still a time-bound concept. Eternity is outside of time completely, so it can't be described in years. Eternity is where there is no time; it's a place of timelessness.

Q: I'm starting to get a headache.

A: I know what you mean. But as mind-stretching as eternity is, it's really a beautiful concept when you think about it. There is so much great stuff to think about when it comes to heaven.

Q: How so?

A: Well, since there is no time in heaven, there is also no aging. We won't age at all. And since there is no aging, there is no dying—which I guess you already knew. And then think of this: there is no time as we know it, but there will be plenty of "time" to do what we want to do. We won't ever be in a hurry.

Q: You're basically saying we can stop and smell the flowers. There will be flowers, right?

A: I'd be very surprised if there were no flowers in heaven.

Q: Not having to rush around does sound great. But why do I have this vague fear that we'll just be floating around with nothing to do—like we'll be bored?

A: You might think that, but it's impossible to be bored in heaven. We'll be so alive that the lives we are living now will seem dead by comparison. But most people don't think of it that way.

Q: Why not?

A: Because it's just hard for us to imagine something as wonderful as heaven. Plus, we get a lot of our worst ideas about heaven from movies. Most movies that portray heaven give you the idea that it's going to be like something out of a depressing existentialist play...produced on a low budget. There always seems to be that dry-ice fog on the ground and maybe a Greek column or two. Who would want to go there? Not me! But I have no doubt that the real thing will be very, very different. Certainly a far cry from our lame images of floating around in the clouds like drugged-up zombies.

Q: What makes you so sure?

A: Two reasons. First, common sense. If the God of the Bible created everything that is fantastic on earth—and he even invented the concept of what we think of as beauty—then whatever he has planned for heaven will be more glorious than what we can imagine. It just stands to reason that the one who invented what we think of as beauty must have something really gorgeous planned for what he calls paradise. The level of joy and meaning in heaven has to be beyond our wildest dreams. The most vivid colors on earth will literally pale in comparison, and everything that amazes us on earth and gives us a sense of hope and fulfillment is nothing but a small foretaste of what's to come. It's hard to take that in, but you can bet it will be the opposite of boring. In some ways it's not so surprising that it's hard for us to imagine—or for movie directors to imagine. It's genuinely beyond us.

Q: You said there were two reasons.

A: The second reason I know heaven will be fantastic is the Bible's description of it. Try to picture what this verse is describing: "Eye hath not seen, nor ear heard, neither have entered into the heart of man, the things which God hath prepared for them that love him."[2]

Q: It's hard to imagine that the passage refers to floating around and being bored.

A: You're not kidding.

Q: You said heaven is outside time, so does that mean everyone will be young in heaven?

A: Yes, but not young in the sense of "not old."

Q: What other kind of young is there?

A: Again, young and old are time-bound concepts. Think of it this way: we will be just as we were always meant to be, perfect and full of life, fuller than we can probably imagine right now.

Q: So we'll have loads of energy and be all hyper?

A: Not hyper but, yes, full of energy! We'll be bursting with life but at perfect peace.

Q: So we'll seem to be young.

A: Yes, in terms of energy and innocence. But in other ways we'll have the attributes that on earth we associate with old age.

Q: You don't mean bursitis. That runs in my family.

A: No, I mean the good things we associate with old age. Things like wisdom and insight and perspective. Imagine someone who has all the energy and life of youth combined with all the wisdom of old age. We don't see that sort of combination in this world, but in heaven that's exactly what we can expect. The best of youth and old age but outside of any particular age. We'll be eternally young but wiser than the oldest, wisest person who ever lived.

We don't know how wise someone would be if he or she lived to be eight hundred years old, or eight thousand, but we have to believe that person would be much wiser than the wisest people who ever lived on earth. God is infinitely wise, so we can't imagine what the limits of wisdom are, but we can guess that we'll be wiser than anything we can imagine right now.

Q: What will heaven look like? You mentioned there won't be fog machines. How about pearly gates?

A: It's hard to be too specific, but one thing I can say for sure is that the idea of Saint Peter standing in front of some pearly gates in the clouds, holding a ledger and figuring out who gets to go in and who takes the express elevator going down, is not in the Bible.

Q: Whoa. Really?

A: Really. It's an instance of somebody pulling something out of context, and somehow it became part of the culture. We talk about it as though it were true, but it's not.

Q: Are you saying there are no pearly gates?

A: There are pearly gates, but it's nothing like we typically imagine. These ideas can get so twisted they have very little relation to the original idea. Here's what the Bible says about pearly gates. In chapter 21 of the book of Revelation, God creates the new heaven and the new earth, which is another conversation entirely. It's the end of the world as we know it, and God creates a heavenly city called the New Jerusalem. It's a city in the classical or medieval sense, so it has a huge wall around it with gates in the wall. The Bible says there are twelve gates, three on the south side, three on the north side, three on the east side, and three on the west side. Each of the gates is made from a single pearl. So the twelve gates are where we get the phrase "pearly gates."

Q: Those are the pearly gates?

A: It's not what you had in mind, am I right? We have come to think of Saint Peter standing in front of an arch looming above two metal gates, like at the front of an estate or something. And of course the scene is floating in the clouds, just as we've seen it in cartoons. But that's not how the Bible describes it. The Bible talks about a walled city with twelve gates, each at a different place in the wall surrounding the heavenly city. Twelve separate gates.

Q: And each gate is made from a single pearl?

A: That's what it says. They'd have to be gigantic. And they'd have to come from oysters about the size of a football field.

Q: I'm getting confused again.

A: Some of the confusion about heaven comes from taking biblical descriptions too literally. The question is, are some of these things metaphors, or are they exact descriptions?

Q: You're asking me?

A: It's a rhetorical question! We can't really know the answer. We know that, given the context, which is the book of Revelation, we are talking about things that are very tough to put in a language that humans can understand. These things are so far beyond us, just as the concept of eternity is beyond us. God is trying to explain it using words, but from our limited, earthbound perspective, we're only capable of getting the basic idea. The Bible talks about streets of gold, for instance.[3] Of course those things could be literal. But when it comes to the gates in the city wall, are we supposed to imagine pearls that are so huge they came from oysters the size of a football field? I tend to think not. It's possible that God, who can make anything and who invented the idea of oysters and pearls and oceans, might have made the pearls without relying on huge oysters. Jesus turned water into wine at a marriage held in Cana—and he skipped the grape part of the process, right? Kind of did an end run around the whole vineyard, so to speak.

Q: I guess so.

A: So maybe God created pearls without using oysters. The bottom line is that we don't know, and it doesn't matter. God can do as he likes, and we can trust him.

Q: So giant oyster or no giant oyster, the bottom line is that the idea of the pearly gates is not what we thought it was?

A: Correct.

Q: Do animals go to heaven when they die?

A: Hard to say for sure, but when I was a kid, there was a cat in our neighborhood that was really mean and would hide in the bushes. When you walked past, especially if you were wearing shorts, he'd *leap* out at you and try to scratch your legs.

Q: Okay...

A: Then he'd scramble away and hiss at you. His name was Smokey. I'm pretty sure we shouldn't expect to see Smokey in heaven.

Smokey used to crawl up under the hood of a car when the engine was still warm, and one time the owner started the car, and Smokey's ear got clipped by the radiator fan. I think that's what embittered him toward life and caused him to wander the neighborhood seeking revenge on our species. But it's just a guess. Poor Smokey!

Q: Er...other than Smokey, do you think animals go to heaven?

A: I don't know. There's nothing in the Bible or in the tradition of the church that tells us much about this one way or the other, so we can't know for sure. We can speculate that they'll be there, and there are reasons to believe they will be, but we can't really know.

Q: But you'd guess they will be?

A: Yes, but it's a guess. Heaven will be glorious in ways we can't imagine, and it seems that every wonderful thing we can imagine will be there. Animals are some of the most vivid examples of God's creativity, and some of them show love and have other qualities that are remarkable. But there are arguments against animals going to heaven too. The main one is based on the teaching that it's the creatures who are made in God's image—human beings—who exist beyond the grave because they have an immortal soul.

Q: So what do I tell my daughter when her turtle dies?

A: Can't you tell her he went to the big Turtle Bowl in the Sky?

Q: Actually, that's what I did tell her. Little Ogden left us last month. He is no more... He's an ex-turtle.

A: I'm so sorry.

Q: Anyway, telling my daughter he went to the big Turtle Bowl in the Sky didn't seem to cut it. Our turtle bowl could get really stinky, so the idea of a giant one in the sky was kind of a disgusting bummer.

A: Reminds me of a friend I had in college who wore a goatee. It was his trademark, but when he showed up at the beginning of his senior year, it was gone. It was hard for some of us to deal with. When any of us asked about it, he comforted us by saying it had gone to that Big Chin in the Sky.

Q: Can we get back to the question of whether animals go to heaven?

A: Of course. We know that heaven won't lack any good thing. We just don't know the specifics of what that means. I'd guess there will be animals in heaven, but we can really only know for sure if the Bible spells it out, and this is one of those things where we're a bit stuck.

Q: But what about the practical side of this: what do you tell a little boy or girl whose pet has died?

A: If you can believe it, this question gets to the heart of all questions. To *the* question…

Q: Are you referring to the meaning of life?

A: Sort of. The question of what to tell your daughter about her late turtle gets to the larger question—what I'm calling *the* question—which is "Who is God?"

Q: I'm not sure I'm following you.

A: Here's the point. There are many questions we can't answer, like the question about where turtles go when they die. But if we know who God is, and if we know that he is who he says he is—trustworthy and loving and all-powerful and all-wise—it changes everything. With all the questions we can't answer satisfactorily, this is the one question we need the answer for. If we understand that God is real, that he is loving beyond our wildest dreams, and that he is on our side, then we can relax and know that we don't have to have the final answer to every little question.

God tells us in the Bible that we shouldn't be troubled about anything, we shouldn't worry.[4] He's not scolding us; he's trying to comfort us, the way a parent comforts a child who's upset. God says that it's all okay, that we can trust him. He uses phrases such as "fear not" and "do not lose heart."[5] Jesus says, "Do not let your hearts be troubled."[6] Over and over God tells us he'll take care of us if we'll let him be in charge. If we'll give him our worries and troubles and questions, he'll take care of things.

Q: And this relates to Little Ogden's whereabouts how, exactly?

A: If we can communicate this fundamental idea about God to our kids—that they can trust God completely about everything in their lives—then it helps them deal with sadness and disappointment and all sorts of hurts in life. If we can get that across to our kids, then we're doing far more than telling them the answer to whether they'll see their turtles in heaven.

Q: You're saying that wondering about whether Little Ogden will be there to greet us when we pass over really gets to a much bigger question?

A: Yes. If we talk about a trustworthy God who loves us, we're giving our kids the answer to the question behind their question. And let's face it, the question behind *all* questions is whether we can trust God. He says emphatically that we really can trust him, that it's the only way to live. So we shouldn't dismiss the questions we have, but until we get answers to those questions, we can rest in the knowledge that we have the ultimate answer in Jesus. God wants us to be intellectually curious—he's the one who put the longing for answers and meaning inside us! He doesn't want us to be content in our ignorance, and he doesn't want us to be afraid to explore the deepest questions we have. But at the same time he wants us to know that when we are confused or questioning, he is with us and loves us.

Q: So some questions are simply too big for earthbound humans?

A: Absolutely. Just as some things are impossible for children to understand, certain things are impossible for even the smartest adult to understand. But God has all the answers and says if we look to him, everything will be okay. And on another level, God himself is the answer to all our questions. God says that when we spend time in his presence, through prayer or worship, somehow our nagging questions and our anxieties evaporate. It's much the same as when a child who has skinned her knee runs to her parent for a hug. The parent's embrace somehow makes everything okay. Even if the bruise or scrape isn't touched, the presence of the parent and the warm hug somehow radically change the situation. That's what it's supposed to be like in our relationship with our heavenly Father. We know everything will be okay because God is there. He wants us to learn to feel his embrace, and that is done through spending time in his presence through prayer. It doesn't come naturally. What comes naturally is anxiety and fretting. But trusting in God and being at peace are supernatural, and that's what prayer allows us to experience.[7] That's a long way from the turtle question, I realize.

Q: No, no. I appreciate it. Can I ask about hamsters?

A: I'm sorry, but we have to move on.

Q: Here's a more-human question: can someone get kicked out of heaven?

A: Only if you get caught chewing gum. I know it sounds odd, but they're extremely strict about that up there.

Q: Ha.

A: Seriously, though, the most authoritative answer seems to be no, we can't get kicked out of heaven.

Q: How did you arrive at that?

A: Well, once we are in heaven—or even if we've gone to hell—we are in an eternal state. We can't ever change that state. But at the same time, it seems that when we are in heaven, we still will have free will.

Q: Why do you think that?

A: We know that in heaven we will love God, and love isn't possible—in heaven or on earth—without free will. It has to be a choice we make. So how can we explain this paradox: we have free will to reject God even while we are in heaven, but we somehow can't reject God while we are in heaven?

Q: Don't look at me; I'm stumped.

A: The answer, I think—and this is philosophical speculation—has to do with the idea that the more you obey God, the more you want to obey God. The more you do his will, the more you desire to do his will.

Q: Okay...

A: It's really pretty interesting. Somehow, by obeying God you make it easier to obey him. I guess it's like exercise.

Q: What?

A: Obeying God is a lot like exercise. When you exercise, it's difficult at first. But every time you do it, you get stronger. The more you exercise, the easier it becomes to exercise. It's always a little bit difficult, but if you push through, you get stronger. Eventually you get so strong that you can't imagine what it was like to be as weak as you were when you started.

Q: Well, if you put it that way, it makes sense.

A: Every time we obey God, it's a choice, but making the right choice gets easier and easier as we continue to make right choices. But to get back to your initial question, the idea behind this is that there eventually comes a point when you almost can't do anything but follow God's will. You reach a point where not doing his will would be so radically and profoundly against everything inside you that it really is practically impossible.

Q: So you can't help but choose to obey God, and yet you're saying you also are free to disobey?

A: Yes. But I imagine that when we are in heaven, we won't dream of disobeying God. A crude analogy would be to say that disobeying God would be like stabbing yourself. You are totally free to do it at any moment, but you don't do it! Why? You simply don't ever want to. And you don't ever get close to wanting to. You are free to do it, but you never would.

Toward the end of his life, C. S. Lewis was married to a poet named Joy Gresham. The movie *Shadowlands* tells the story of their relationship and of Joy's death from cancer. During the painful mourning for his beloved wife, Lewis reminded himself of what he had written about years earlier. He firmly believed that this world is but a shadow of the world ahead of us and that the world ahead of us will be far more real than anything we've yet experienced. We can't know the answers to all the questions that trouble us in this life, but we can know the answer to the one question that's behind all other questions.

14

Do Good Deeds Get Us into Heaven?

Faith vs. Works; Serving God; God's Will for Your Future; Dutch Preaching

At one time or another we've all felt that we simply can't do enough. And if you ever compare yourself to the eighteenth-century composer Johann Sebastian Bach, you'll feel this way as never before. Bach was about as prolific as anyone who has ever lived. Journalist Terry Mattingly says, "Bach was astonishingly busy.... [He oversaw] the music in four Leipzig churches...and had 20 children. He taught music lessons and Latin classes. He rehearsed and performed his own organ works and directed the local boys' choirs."[1] Besides all this, Bach was one of the most prolific composers in history. Among other things, he wrote a new thirty-minute cantata each week to be performed that Sunday in church. It's all rather dizzying.

One secret to Bach's productivity may lie in two tiny notations he put at the beginning and ending of his compositions. When he started writing, he wrote the initials J. J., an abbreviation of the Latin phrase *Jesu Juva.* At the end he would write S. D. G., which stood for

Soli Deo Gloria. The first notation meant "Jesus, help me." The second meant "May all the glory be to God."

Q: Here's a tough one. Is having faith in God more important than being a good person?

A: It depends on what you mean by "being a good person."

Q: Just generally doing good and being good toward others.

A: That's what I thought you meant. This is a hugely important question. In church history it has been referred to as the "faith versus works" controversy. Over the centuries there's been a lot of theological debate on this question.

Q: What does "faith versus works" mean?

A: Just as your question implies, some people say God is mostly interested in our having faith in him, so that's the "faith" side of the argument. Others say it's all about what we do, or don't do, and traditionally that has been referred to as doing "good works"—or just "works."

Q: So which is more important?

A: Like all of the big questions, it's a big question because there's a lot to it. Before I try to answer it, can I give you some background?

Q: I can't stop you.

A: About five hundred years ago in a German monastery in the town of Wittenberg, a certain Martin Luther started thinking seriously about this issue of faith and works. Maybe you've heard of him?

Q: The name does ring a bell. Unless I've got him mixed up with Ricky Martin and that other Luther guy.

A: Luther Vandross?

Q: No, the one from 2 Live Crew. Never mind.

A: The Luther I'm talking about was a German monk in the early 1500s. One day he was in his cell studying the New Testament. He was reading the book of Romans when he landed on this verse: "For in the gospel a righteousness from God is revealed, a righteousness that is by faith from first to last, just as it is written: 'The righteous will live by faith.' "[2] The words hit him as they never had before, and from that day onward Martin Luther and the world would never be the same.

Q: Why is that?

A: That phrase "the righteous will live by faith" made him realize that God's view of us has to do primarily with our faith, not our behavior. Behavior has to be secondary, because behavior can be faked. Much of what Luther had seen in the Christianity of his day emphasized behavior. If you committed such and such a sin, you'd be on your way to hell. If you did such and such a good deed, it was said to move you closer to heaven.

But that day, reading the first chapter of Romans, Luther saw that it was a person's faith in God that mattered. We could do all the right things outwardly but still close our hearts to Jesus and our fellowman. Or we could do the right things but for selfish reasons: out of fear or the desire to preserve the status quo or the hope of getting ahead or the desire to impress other people. But Luther realized that God looked at our hearts, not at our actions. We can't fool God. He can see our faith in him or our lack of faith. And that was what mattered.

Q: So Luther landed on the "faith" side of the controversy.

A: You could almost say that he *invented* the faith side of the controversy. He realized that without this understanding of faith, a person could assume that it's possible to earn your way into heaven, which is a heretical idea. If we can earn our way into heaven, we don't need God's grace. We don't need Jesus to die on the cross for our sins. If it's all about our behavior and good deeds, it's all about us and not about God.

Q: But don't most people believe that if you're good—or if your good deeds outweigh your bad deeds—you'll make it into heaven?

A: I know that's a common belief, but it's not Christianity. Christianity is the one religion that says we can't impress God by doing good deeds. We can't earn our way into heaven and shouldn't even try. We should turn to Jesus, and he will open the door to heaven for us, but through *his* moral perfection. God's love for us is never based on our behavior. God loves the worst sinner the same as the most holy saint. His unconditional love is at the core of Christianity.

Q: You're serious when you say Christianity is the only religion that doesn't judge us according to our good or bad deeds?

A: That's right. No other religion has this view of God's grace. When Martin Luther read the first chapter of Romans, he realized we could never be morally perfect, which you might think would doom us to hell. But that's where God's grace comes in. Even when we fail, if we look to Jesus and his sacrifice for us, we will be forgiven for our failures. And having been forgiven, we are welcomed into God's kingdom. That's what Luther discovered that changed not only his life but the church's understanding of the centrality of faith.

Q: But it seems to make more sense to a lot of people that it's up to them to live the right kind of life.

A: On some level that idea appeals to a lot of people. But think about what that belief leads to. If Christianity were mostly about our behavior, we would think we could earn our way into heaven. That idea leads to self-righteousness and the tendency to judge those who aren't as "moral" as we are.

But true Christianity levels the playing field. It teaches that we *all* fall short of the glory of God. We are all sinners.

We all need God's grace and forgiveness.[3] There are no second-class citizens in the kingdom of God. We *all* need God's grace, and he loves each one of us equally and with no conditions attached. He welcomes us into his kingdom based on our simple and humble faith in him, not based on anything we've done or chosen not to do. No one who reaches out to God in faith is rejected.

Q: But earlier you were talking about God's holiness and saying that he can't tolerate anything that isn't holy. Doesn't that mean that moral behavior is important to him?

A: Of course God wants us to obey him, which translates into moral behavior. But Luther saw that good deeds and obedience to God are ultimately not the most important things. We all need to do good things. Remember, God commands us to love others, to serve others, to put the interests of others ahead of our own priorities. And that's just the beginning. But it's even more important that we understand that ultimately we are moral failures who will never get anywhere close to achieving perfection. That means we have no hope of getting into heaven without Jesus. Jesus' sacrifice for us is the only thing that can save us.

Jesus was morally perfect when he lived on earth, and when he died, he exchanged his perfection for our sin. The Bible says, "God made him who had no sin to be sin for us."[4] The doctrine that grew out of the teaching that we depend only on Jesus for our salvation, which Luther discovered when he read Romans 1:17, is called *sola fide,* which is Latin for "only faith."

Q: Does this let us off the hook when it comes to doing good deeds? Can we simply have faith and then go ape? Do as we like?

A: Um, no. Just as we can't fake our way into heaven by doing good deeds, neither can we fake genuine faith. If we have faith in Jesus—if we really understand how much he loves us—our lives can't help but reflect that faith. Genuine faith naturally leads to an obedient life. If we have faith, it will be obvious in our behavior.

So if a person says he has become a Christian but his life doesn't show evidence of that, there is good reason to question the genuineness of his faith. You can't lie or cheat or steal or treat your family and co-workers poorly and then say that your behavior doesn't matter, that only your faith matters. If your life does not reflect the love of God, then how can you say you have faith in God?[5] Anyone who claims God's grace but consistently behaves no differently than someone without faith doesn't understand faith.

Q: Okay, then good deeds, or what you are calling "works," do come into the picture.

A: Yes. But only as an outgrowth of faith in Jesus. In the book of James, we read that "faith by itself, if it is not accompanied by action, is dead,"[6] meaning that if people's lives don't show evidence of faith, it's entirely possible they don't have faith! Real faith will always produce good works. So just because people intellectually agree with what the Bible says, it doesn't mean they really believe. Faith can't just be in our heads. It has to be in the totality of who we are, so it will be visible somehow.

You could almost say faith and works are two sides of the same coin. If we allow Jesus to come into our lives by faith, we will begin evincing the sort of behavior God wants us to have. It's not fakery; it's real. Our behavior follows our faith in God.

Q: I've known people who claim to be "born again" but lack kindness, love, and concern for others. How do you explain that?

A: They forgot to take their meds?

Q: Seriously.

A: I'd say those sorts of people fundamentally misunderstand what it means to have faith in Jesus. They reduce faith to something smaller than it really is, to an idea in their head. They think that grasping the "idea" of faith is enough.

But if a person's head and heart truly believe something, that person's life will follow. If you really have faith, you will want to do the things that God commands. Of course no one is perfect, and even a person with very strong faith will stumble and make mistakes. But their attitude will be different. There will be a humility, because they understand it's about how wonderful Jesus is, not about how wonderful they are.

Q: So you don't hold out hope that anyone could ever live a completely moral life?

A: Even with the world's strongest faith, it won't happen this side of heaven. If we have real faith in Jesus, we are going to change, but it's a gradual, lifelong process. Along the way we will continue to sin and fail, but God is there to forgive us and love us and accept us, no matter how far we fall short. At the same time, if someone is putting his or her life in God's hands, that person will grow to be more and more like Jesus. This process is called "sanctification," which means "becoming holy." One of the surest signs of faith is seeing people acknowledge their problems and shortcomings and begin to deal with them.

Q: Okay, let's say I want to believe in Jesus.

A: Okay, let's.

Q: Can't I just live a quiet life, or do I have to "serve God" in some big way? I get hung up on the idea of "serving God." It just seems so daunting, like it's not for me.

A: Everybody has different ideas of what it means to serve God. I had a friend who said he wanted to serve God—but in an advisory capacity. But seriously, what is it about serving God that you think is so daunting?

Q: It's the idea that if you serve God, you lose control of your life. God might tell you to become a priest or a nun or a missionary or something, and you'd have to do it!

A: If God knows you intimately—and he does, since he created you—then he knows exactly what he made you for, and he'll never ask you to do something you're not equipped to do with his help. You can trust God to send you in the direction that fits precisely who you are. He doesn't want to ruin your life; he wants to help you live the life he *created* you for. But to find out what that life is, you first have to surrender your will to his purposes for you.

Q: But how do you explain all those ghastly tales of martyrs suffering excruciating torture and dying awful deaths on iron grills and things? I heard a lot of those stories when I was a kid, and ever since, I've felt like I could never go down that path.

A: You think that serving God necessarily leads to being martyred?

Q: I guess the idea did kind of cross my mind.

A: God calls people to do what he has prepared them to do, and extremely few are called to martyrdom. It's not that if you decide to follow God, you'd better be prepared to do the very thing you'd most hate doing. God doesn't amuse himself by making us miserable. Instead, he has something for each one of us that is unique, and it's designed just for that person. He gives a person all the gifts needed to do whatever he calls the person to do.

Q: So I shouldn't question whether I'm cut out to serve God?

A: Of course not. Every human being was *created* to serve God!

Q: And I don't need to worry that serving God might involve having to be a missionary in some buggy jungle—or dying a gruesome death?

A: Anything's possible, but if I were you, I definitely would not worry about it. What you should worry about is the idea of *resisting* God's purposes in your life. Resisting his calling for you will cause more pain and difficulty than giving yourself over to his will. That's for sure.

Q: How could avoiding this big unknown—what you have referred to as "the will of God"—be more difficult than simply sticking with what's familiar? I'm not sure what you're getting at.

A: Because doing God's will means you get to do the one thing you were built for. Ultimately, serving God is the only thing worth doing, because it's the reason each one of us was put on earth. God isn't planning anything for you that he hasn't planned for you *specifically*, knowing exactly who you are and what you are capable of. Serving God involves trusting that he loves you and knows what is best for you.

Q: But let's say that even the slim possibility that God might want me to be a celibate monk or to take a vow of poverty or silence is enough to keep me from serving him. What then?

A: I'd say if you allow such an unlikely event to keep you from God, you'd be cheating yourself out of the best life you could possibly have. God is the only one who can unlock your real potential, because he's the one who put it inside you! It's hard to overstate this, but serving God really is the one thing you can't mess up. He created you to serve him. Everything else you might try is *more* difficult, not less difficult. You won't find meaning and purpose and fulfillment until you submit your will to God's will.

Do you remember Eric Liddell from the old movie *Chariots of Fire*?

Q: I think I saw it on video.

A: He's the Olympic champion who refused to run on Sunday and ended up being a huge national hero. He knew that God had created him to run—and to run fast—and he said, "When I run, I feel God's pleasure." He knew there was a deep joy at the heart of serving God, even when things got difficult. God doesn't call us to be anything outside of who he created us to be. There's a book on this subject titled *The Call*, by Os Guinness, that you might want to check out. And I don't think it mentions any martyrs, in case you were worried about that.

Q: So God might want me to be a track star?

A: I wouldn't bet on it, but anything's possible! The point is that whatever he's calling you to do, he wants you to do it to his glory, and he'll be with you every step of the way, no pun intended. He asks us to turn our careers and our relationships and our futures—everything—over to him. Many people experience miracles when they turn their lives over to God. So the only question is "how" to serve God, never "if." Serving God brings genuine joy, never drudgery and never fear. When we live our lives for his glory, we "feel the Lord's pleasure."

So forget the idea that serving God means a life in "religious work" or "ministry." Not everyone is called to a life in the ministry or on the mission field. Think about all the people who have served God in tremendous ways but *weren't* priests or missionaries.

Q: Can you give me some examples? I think nine or ten should do it.

A: That's awfully specific. Let's see. There was Jackie Robinson, who played baseball. Of course Sir Isaac Newton was a scientist. Johann Sebastian Bach was a composer. T. S. Eliot was a poet, as was Dante, of course. Lillian Gish was an actress. William Wilberforce was an abolitionist and politician. Flannery O'Connor wrote fiction. Rosa Parks was a civil-rights pioneer. John Jay was the first chief justice of the United States Supreme Court. Rembrandt was a painter. Is that enough?

Q: That should hold me for a while. And all of them were really serious Christians?

A: Without question. And there's not a missionary or martyr in the lot. God called them to serve him in other capacities. I don't know about you, but I'm awfully glad they didn't spend their lives as preachers.

Q: I know what you mean. Rembrandt probably would have preached in Dutch, and I can't understand a word of it!

A: Right! That's the problem with Dutch preaching. If you don't know Dutch, you're stuck!

Q: Okay, those eleven people are pretty interesting characters. So you think God might call me to do something like one of them?

A: I don't see why not!

Q: Like maybe I could discover gravity the way Newton did! Or break the color barrier in baseball like Jackie Robinson—or write the Divine Comedy like Dante? Or star in D. W. Griffith's The Birth of a Nation?

A: Er, I'm afraid all of those things have already been done—by the folks just mentioned. They can really only be done once. After that, they kind of lose their sizzle.

Q: Oh.

A: But I'm sure God has something in store for you. He created each of us to serve him in a way that no one else can, since each of us is unique. And whatever it is, you can know he's given you the ability to do it. And of course God does call *some* people into ministry. We don't want to pretend that's not possible.

Q: I just don't see myself learning Dutch!

A: You'll figure it out.

It seems obvious that God gave Johann Sebastian Bach an extraordinary ability to write music. But Bach knew his talent alone wasn't enough; he needed God's help every time he began composing. Bach also knew that when he finished a piece—as proud as he might be of what he'd accomplished—both he and the music had been brought into existence to glorify God, and God alone.

15

Is Jesus Really Coming Back?

The King's Return; Do Miracles Still Happen?; Fairy Tales

About seven hundred years before Jesus was born, a blind Greek poet named Homer wrote the classic works known as *The Iliad* and *The Odyssey.* In *The Iliad,* Odysseus and his Cephallenians sail to the fabled city of Troy to fight the ten-year-long Trojan War. But in *The Odyssey,* the war is over, and Odysseus begins his long and adventurous journey home, taking another ten years. During all this time his wife, Penelope, waits for him.

There are suitors who want to marry Penelope and become king of Ithaca. They move into Odysseus's palace, eating his food and blackening his name at every opportunity. They tell Penelope that Odysseus will never come back and that if by some miracle he's still alive, he has certainly forgotten all about her. But Penelope is a picture of faithfulness against all odds. She continues to hold off the suitors, waiting for the king to return home. She knows that when he finally comes back, all things will be restored, and justice will at last be meted out.

And as people have been reading for twenty-seven centuries, Odysseus does indeed return. Upon landing, he disguises himself in the rags of a beggar. But in a scene that seems as contemporary as anything we can imagine, Odysseus's ancient dog, Argos, recognizes him instantly. Argos has waited his whole life for his master to come home. His old ears prick up, and his tail wags once more. His lifelong hopes have at last been realized, and having been again patted on the head by the one who greeted his entrance into the world, he can depart it in peace, and does. When Odysseus returns to the palace, he kills all the suitors who have tormented his long-suffering wife. They can no longer sneer at the king's delayed return or take liberties in his home. And his wife and his son and all those who have waited for the return of their king are not disappointed.

The theme of return—especially of the return of a king who has been away for a long, long time—is a popular and powerful one in literature. Is it possible that the reason for its popularity and power is that there is a real King who has promised to return and to restore justice? He will embrace those who have been waiting and waiting, and they will recognize him when at long last he arrives again.

Q: Is Jesus really coming back?

A: Of course not. He just wants us to feel like he might so we don't get too far out of line in his absence. Like when a teacher has to leave the room for a few minutes!

Q: Say what?

A: Obviously I'm kidding! But so many people have a bad idea of who God is that they really think of his return as a bad thing instead of as the most glorious thing they could ever imagine. So they don't want him to come back any more than they want the teacher to show up! It's pretty tragic.

Q: Why do you think Christians talk so much about Jesus' return?

A: Mainly because Jesus talked about it a lot himself, and Jesus didn't exactly say things just for effect! So Christians talk about it because it's true.

Q: What do you mean?

A: I mean he's really coming back. It's part of the whole package of core Christian beliefs. And we do want to be prepared, no?

Q: Prepared for what? It all still sounds pretty scary, like I'm going to get in trouble.

A: For having fun? For enjoying life? The idea that God is against our enjoying life is one of the worst lies ever perpetrated on the human race. It's probably responsible for more people missing out on a relationship with God than we would care to imagine. Of course God *is* against our committing injustice toward others, and he's against our hurting others—and ourselves. So, yes, Jesus' return does mean that injustices and evil will be exposed. But why wouldn't we want God to restore justice and deal with evil? If we're not looking forward to it, we should ask ourselves *why* we're not.

Q: Okay, let's say I am looking forward to it. But for two thousand years Christians have been saying Jesus is about to come back, and so far we're still waiting.

A: Well, again, Jesus himself said it very clearly, and he wasn't exactly the sort to blow smoke to impress a crowd. We're not talking about P. T. Barnum here. And the belief that Jesus will return to earth is in the Nicene Creed, along with all the other fundamentals of the faith, so it's not some optional, fringe belief that you only hear on religious radio programs at three in the morning.

Q: But can't the idea of Jesus' return just be a nice idea without people having to accept it as literal fact?

A: Well, it *is* a great idea and one that is good to think about. But it's far more than a great idea; it's also *true.* Sunsets and children are nice ideas too, and both of them actually exist. And even if you think the idea of Jesus coming back is a lousy idea, it's still true. Just because Christians have been expecting him to return for two thousand years doesn't mean it's not going to happen.

Q: But why should this be so important to people?

A: Because for those who know Jesus and love him, it's a profound hope, one that people long for in the deepest part of their hearts. If you really know him, you know that he is the answer to your grief and to the world's brokenness. The idea that he is returning, that he'll put an end to injustice and suffering, is the deepest and fondest wish of the human race. Our King is coming back to rescue us, to bring joy back to a pain-racked world. It's the real fairy tale of which all the others are echoes. We need to know that the King is returning, really. God wants us to have that hope, to encourage us along the way.

Q: But Jesus was crucified two thousand years ago. Why wouldn't he already have come back if it was going to happen?

A: Think about how long it took Jesus to come the first time. All through the Old Testament, God promises that he will send his Messiah, the anointed one, to be the Savior of the world. The Israelites believed this for centuries, and they talked about it and waited for it. And many doubted that it would ever happen. Cynicism wasn't invented in 1981. And they had an even better reason to doubt, because the Messiah had never come before. But Christians know that he really did come eventually. The unbelievable came true.

Q: It "came true" if you happen to believe Jesus was the Messiah. But not everyone does.

A: Well, that's another conversation. But if you are a Christian and you've looked at the evidence, you know that he did come and that he fulfilled the hundreds of Old Testament prophecies. And he fulfilled the one prophecy that would seem to be the hardest of all: he brought light to the Gentiles.

Q: Please translate that.

A: Jesus brought the God of the universe, the one the Israelites worshiped, to the rest of the world. The terms *gentiles* and *heathen* simply mean the nations outside of Israel. They had been worshiping all kinds of idols and had no idea there was a God who created the universe and who had created them and who loved them. Until the time of Jesus, only Israel knew and worshiped the one true God. But God said that someday he would send his Messiah, who would come out of Israel and who would do something that had never been done before: he would bring the salvation of God to the whole world. He would be a "light to the Gentiles."[1]

Q: Okay...

A: And that's exactly what Jesus did! Who can deny that the God who was previously known only to the nation of Israel is now worshiped by people all over the globe? I'd call that a miracle. People on every continent and in each of the nearly two hundred countries on the planet worship the God of Israel. And it's through the Messiah, Jesus, that it happened—just as Isaiah the prophet had said hundreds of years before Jesus was born.

Q: It's certainly intriguing...

A: Now that we've seen that the Messiah came the first time, as was promised—and he did just what the Scriptures said he would do—why should we doubt that he'll come back? Remember, the Messiah said he would return, and it wasn't an offhand comment that we are overinterpreting or a vague half statement that we are teasing into something larger. It was all quite clear.[2]

Q: You called it a "miracle" that people around the world now worship the God of Israel. Do you think actual miracles still happen today?

A: How do you mean?

Q: Somehow I can believe in miracles that happened two thousand years ago. But believing they can happen today is another story.

A: Why?

Q: It's much easier for me to imagine Jesus walking on water or turning water into wine in the distant past, before technology and major advances in science, when everything was simpler. But the idea of such things happening in a world of mp3s and cell phones and the Mars rover doesn't seem possible.

A: I hear what you're saying, but you're not being logical!

Q: Why isn't that logical?

A: Because you're really saying the period in which Jesus lived, two thousand years ago, was somehow not real. But it was every bit as real as today or yesterday.

Q: What do you mean?

A: You're romanticizing the past. In your mind you are turning a historical period into a kind of hazy, distant, fairy-tale world, where *anything* could happen—miracles included. But if you make it that, then we're back where we started.

Q: Which is where?

A: In a place where the God of the Bible is not really who he says he is but is just a vague, fairy-tale kind of God who does stuff in fairy-tale worlds but not in *this* world, someone who doesn't do things in the world of history and facts and figures and real flesh-and-blood people.

Q: I'm not sure I'm following.

A: You have to decide whether God is real or not. When you say miracles could have happened in a distant time and place but not now, what you're really saying is that the distant past was fundamentally different than today. You're saying that it was a kind of fairy-tale nonreality and that God was doing things but only in a fairy-tale world. That isn't the case at all. The ancient world was as real as our world. It was just like our reality.

Q: But I didn't say anything about a fairy-tale world.

A: Not using those words, but you're saying that God intervenes only in that hazy, distant world that doesn't have any real bearing on our world today. And you're treating the real world of two thousand years ago as though kooky things could happen—sick people could be healed, and dead people could come back to life—but you don't believe those same things can occur today.

Q: Now that you mention it, that is sort of how I think about it.

A: A lot of people do. It's as if they start out with a childhood faith that never really matures. As they grow up and learn about the world, they banish all this God stuff to that faraway fairy-tale world, a world where anything can happen, where Santa can exist and the tooth fairy can exist.

But we have to understand that if the things in the Bible aren't *entirely* real, they're not real at all. They can't have a truncated reality that is meaningful only in a faraway realm. They are either genuinely true in all circumstances, or they are merely fairy tales and should be dismissed just as we dismiss Santa Claus. Actually, there's a great book on this subject called *Total Truth,* by Nancy Pearcey. She shows that our culture has relegated God and everything about him to a separate "spiritual realm" that doesn't really touch the world we live in. By doing that we confuse everything and dismiss the reality of God from our lives.[3] But it's intellectually dishonest.

As interesting as it might be to talk about God in theoretical terms, ultimately you have to consider God on his own terms and either accept or reject who he says he is. We're *not* talking about Santa Claus or the tooth fairy. We're talking about someone who either created the universe and continues to sustain life on earth or whose work is limited to a long-ago, fairy-tale-like world. Either Jesus is God in human flesh and he came to earth to die an undeserved death to pay the price of your sins and mine, or he didn't. Either Jesus rose bodily from the dead so that you and I can spend eternity in the presence of God, or he didn't.

If God is who he says he is—and we accept that and put our trust in him—then it makes all the difference in the world.

Stories are important. Fairy tales, myths, and epic poems are a distillation of reality in which the truth, like cream, is skimmed from the top and served to us on a giant's silver spoon. As we hear the story of Jesus, the literal truth of it is vitally important, as are the theological details. But we must not let the details obscure the story's heartbreaking beauty. After we have settled ourselves on the many details, what do we make of the poem at the center of it all, of the glorious, golden dream of a God falling like a star from the heavens to walk upon a planet he invented to rescue it from self-destruction?

Notes

Chapter 1

1. N. T. Wright discussed this idea in a lecture presented in New York City on October 21, 2006. The lecture is available on audio CD from Socrates in the City, www.socratesinthe city.com.
2. See Psalm 90:4; 2 Peter 3:8; Genesis 1:1–2; John 1:1–2.
3. See Genesis 17:3–8 (Abram renamed Abraham); John 1:40–42 (Simon renamed Peter).
4. Luke 11:2, KJV.
5. Psalm 118:26.
6. Matthew 21:9.
7. See Exodus 20:7.
8. See James 2:19.
9. See Exodus 3:4–6, 10, 13–14.
10. See Genesis 12:1–2 (God calls Abram to leave his homeland) and Exodus 3:4 (God speaks to Moses).

Chapter 2

1. See, for example, Exodus 34:6; Nehemiah 9:17; Psalm 103:8.
2. Luke 13:4.
3. Luke 13:5.
4. See Matthew 7:1–5.
5. *Annie Hall,* screenplay by Woody Allen and Marshall Brickman, directed by Woody Allen (Culver City, CA: United Artists, 1977).

Chapter 3

1. The author got this story directly from B. J. Weber.
2. See Deuteronomy 4:23–24; Isaiah 33:14; Hebrews 12:28–29.
3. See 2 Corinthians 5:21.
4. See 2 Samuel 6:6–7.

Chapter 4

1. For more on this idea, see Thomas Howard, *Chance or the Dance?* (San Francisco: Ignatius Press, 2001).
2. For more on false assertions contained in biology textbooks, see James P. Gills, MD, and Tom Woodward, *Darwinism Under the Microscope: How Recent Scientific Evidence Points to Divine Design* (Lake Mary, FL: Charisma House, 2002), 11.
3. For more on the falsification of the fossil record, go to http://evolution-facts.org/Ev-Crunch/c17.htm/; www.bible.ca/tracks/textbook-fraud-dawn-horse-eohippus.htm#horses/; and www.case-creation.org.uk/palae1.html.
4. For more on this idea, see Gills and Woodward, *Darwinism Under the Microscope,* 114–15.

Chapter 5

1. See 1 Corinthians 15:45.
2. Exodus 20:13.
3. See John 21:8–12.
4. See Luke 24:42, KJV.

Chapter 6

1. Lord Melbourne, What Quote, www.whatquote.com/quotes/Lord-Melbourne/26128-Things-are-coming-to.htm.

2. Psalm 139:13.
3. Psalm 139:16.
4. Psalm 139:14.
5. Exodus 21:22–25.
6. Jeremiah 1:5.
7. See Luke 1:41.
8. Luke 1:41–42.
9. The establishment clause is found in the First Amendment to the U.S. Constitution. See www.usconstitution.net/const .html.
10. The text of Thomas Jefferson's letter to the Baptists of Danbury, Connecticut, can be found at www.usconstitution.net/ jeffwall.html.
11. The John Adams quote is found in his "Letter to the Officers of the First Brigade of the Third Division of the Militia of Massachusetts," October 11, 1798. The full quote is as follows: "We have no government armed with power capable of contending with human passions unbridled by morality and religion. Avarice, ambition, revenge or gallantry would break the strongest cords of our Constitution as a whale goes through a net. Our Constitution is designed only for a moral and religious people. It is wholly inadequate for any other." Quote found at www.quotationspage.com/quotes/John_ Adams.

Chapter 7

1. Janie Bradford and Berry Gordy Jr., "Money," copyright © 1959, Longitude Music, BMI.
2. See Matthew 19:23–24.

3. See Proverbs 3:13–14; 8:10, 18–19; 16:16.
4. See Matthew 6:24, KJV.
5. See Matthew 6:19–20.
6. Matthew 6:19–20.
7. 1 Timothy 6:10.
8. See Matthew 21:12–13.
9. "Hercules and the Wagoner," *Aesop's Fables,* www.aesopfables.com/cgi/aesop1.cgi?2&HerculesandtheWagoner.
10. See 2 Thessalonians 3:6–10.
11. Matthew 22:21, KJV.

Chapter 8

1. See Genesis 1:26–27; 2:23–24.
2. See Romans 3:23; 6:23; Ephesians 2:8–9.
3. See Hebrews 4:14–15.

Chapter 9

1. See, for example, Matthew 19:3–9.
2. Matthew 19:4–6.
3. Matthew 19:6, KJV.
4. Matthew 19:8.
5. Matthew 19:9.
6. See Matthew 5:43–45.

Chapter 10

1. See, for example, John Noble Wilford, "Findings: A Cold, Hard Explanation for a Biblical Feat," *New York Times,* April 4, 2006, Science Desk.

2. "The Nicene Creed," from *The Book of Common Prayer* (New York: The Church Hymnal Corporation, 1979), 358–59.

Chapter 11

1. See Philippians 2:6–8.
2. See Matthew 26:36–39.
3. See Romans 5:6–8.
4. Luke 23:35.
5. Romans 8:28, ESV.
6. See Philippians 4:6–7.

Chapter 12

1. See Matthew 28:1–10; Mark 16:1–6; Luke 24:36–43; John 21:1–14; 1 Corinthians 15:3–8.
2. 1 Corinthians 15:14, 17.
3. See 1 Corinthians 15:3–8.
4. For more on the resurrection and other Christian teachings, see John R. W. Stott, *Basic Christianity* (Westchester, IL: InterVarsity Press, 2007).

Chapter 13

1. C. S. Lewis, *The Great Divorce: A Dream* (San Francisco: HarperSanFrancisco, 2001), 20.
2. 1 Corinthians 2:9, KJV.
3. See Revelation 21:21.
4. See Philippians 4:6–7.
5. See, for example, Joshua 8:1, KJV; Jeremiah 51:46; Luke 18:1; Hebrews 12:3.

6. John 14:1.
7. See Philippians 4:6–7.

Chapter 14

1. Terry Mattingly, "When Did Bach Find Time to Pray?" *Adoremus Bulletin* (online edition), 6, no. 8 (November 2000), www.adoremus.org/11-00-mattingly.html.
2. Romans 1:17.
3. See Romans 3:23; 6:23; 5:8; 1 John 1:8–9; Ephesians 2:8–9.
4. 2 Corinthians 5:21.
5. See James 2:14, 17.
6. James 2:17.

Chapter 15

1. Isaiah 49:6, KJV. See also Luke 2:30–32.
2. See John 14:3–4; Matthew 24:36–44.
3. For more on this idea, see Nancy Pearcey, *Total Truth: Liberating Christianity from Its Cultural Captivity* (Wheaton, IL: Crossway Books, 2004).